...663. He is a corresponding member
Spain of the Mallarmé Academy in Paris; the International
Ponzen Academy in Naples; the North American Academy of
the Spanish Language in New York, and the World Academy
of Arts and Culture, of which he is also *Doctor Honoris
Causa*. He is a member of the International Committee of the
World Congresses of Poets and a founding member of the
European Poetry Festival in Leuven, Belgium.

His poetry has been translated into 27 languages. For his
verse and his essays, he has won 20 international prizes,
among which the following are outstanding: the International
Grand Prize of the Swedish Academy, 1972; the Fastenrath
Award of the Spanish Royal Academy, 1977; the Biennial
Award of the Swedish Writers' Association, 1977, the Brussels
Gold Medal of French Culture, 1981; the Gustavo Adolfo
Bécquer Medal of Honour, 1984, the Zeus Cultural Award
(Athens) 1985, and in 1986, the European Literature Prize
(Yugoslavia) for his poetry.

Louis Bourne was born in Virginia, USA in 1942. He received
degrees from the University of North Carolina and Hollins
College, Virginia and an MA in English literature from
Oxford University. Former editor of *The Carolina Quarterly*,
he has lived in Madrid for the last twenty years. Apart from
many translations of the work of Spanish poets, he has trans-
lated the following volumes: *The Crackling Sun* (1981), poems
of Vicente Aleixandre; *The Circles of Hell* (1981), a bilingual
edition of poems by Justo Jorge Padrón; *Quartz* (1987) by the
same poet; and *Selected Poems* (1987) by María Victoria
Atencia. Himself a poet, he has had published two books of
poetry in Spanish and poems in English magazines. He also
edited an anthology in Spanish of 'vertical poetry' by
Argentine poet Roberto Juarroz, and serves as Associate
Editor of Madrid's multi-lingual poetry journal, *Equivalences*.

Justo Jorge Padrón

ON THE CUTTING EDGE

SELECTED POEMS
by
JUSTO JORGE PADRÓN

Translated from the Spanish
by
LOUIS BOURNE

FOREST BOOKS
LONDON ✶ 1988 ✶ BOSTON

PUBLISHED BY FOREST BOOKS
20 Forest View, Chingford, London E4 7AY, U.K.
61 Lincoln Road, Wayland, MA 01788, U.S.A.

First published 1988

Typeset in Great Britain by Cover to Cover, Cambridge
Printed in Great Britain by A. Wheaton & Co. Ltd, Exeter

British Library Cataloguing in Publication Data:
Padrón, Justo Jorge
On the cutting edge: collected poems.
I. Title   II. Bourne, Louis
861'.64   PQ6666.A33
ISBN 0–948259–42–6

Library of Congress Catalogue Card No.:
87–082774

Contents

Acknowledgements

Some of these translations, occasionally in earlier versions,
appeared in the following journals:

Equivalences (Madrid, 1982)
Indian Literature (New Delhi, 1984)
International Poets (Madras, 1986)
Poet (Madras, 1981; special issue on Padrón's poetry)
Stand (Newcastle-on-Tyne, U.K., 1981)

and in the following books and anthologies:

East–West Winds (Mangalore, India, 1982)
Fifth World Congress of Poets (San Francisco, 1981)
Friends Foreign Poetry
(Fourth World Congress of Poets, Seoul, 1979)
Insula, Charles Carrere, Mimmo Morina,
Justo Jorge Padrón (Luxembourg, 1983)
Mystery and Matter
(Fourth European Festival of Poetry, Leuven, Belgium, 1982)
New Directions 43 (New York, 1981)
Poets and Poetry from Europe 1950–1980
(European Festival of Poetry, Leuven, Belgium, 1980)
Quartz, Justo Jorge Padrón (Luxembourg, 1987)
The Circles of Hell (1973–75),
Justo Jorge Padrón (Luxembourg, 1981)
Voices International (Madras, 1982)
World Poetry 2. Poetry Europe (Madras, 1982).

The bilingual edition of *The Circles of Hell* is distributed
by Forest Books.

An earlier version of the Introduction appeared in *NEeuropa*
(N. 35–36, Luxembourg 1981)

The poetry journal *Equivalences* is supported by the
Fernando Rielo Foundation.

All the translations were made in close collaboration with the author.

Introduction
Waters of Sunlight and Despair

In the last few years, Spanish publishers have started to edit collected works of some of the best-known young Spanish poets, so it is gradually becoming easier to assess the contributions of the different poets whose first wave was the so-called 'Venetians' or 'culturalists' dating from Pere Gimferrer's *Arde el mar* (The Sea Blazes, 1966).

Justo Jorge Padrón belongs to what might be called the second wave, two of whose outstanding members are Antonio Colinas and Jaime Siles. Colinas has continued the culturalist style of the early work of Carnero by using the dramatic monologue of an historical figure when he is not waxing sensual and languid in the ruins of classical culture, though recent work ponders the 'starry void'. The intellectual Jaime Siles develops poetic thought in sensuous form. Padrón, however, is more varied and fitful than either of these two and his work does not share the aesthetic distancing that is characteristic of the culturalists. He can be neo-romantic like Colinas, but his poetry is essentially a consideration of personal experience, and, in this respect, occasionally recalls the meditative lyricism of Francisco Brines, a poet of the 1950s. Padrón's second book is dedicated to him.

Yet whereas for Brines time inevitably leads to death and nothingness, and he accepts this condition with a certain stoic fatalism, Padrón's perspective is more vigorous and more cosmic in its searching. Time is no less the destroyer for Padrón, but his poetry begins in the struggle between his visions of a black future and his dreams of salvation in a woman's arms or the ideal beauty of nature. His poems vary from hope to desolation according to the obsession of his mood. The grimness of death is there but attenuated by the refuge and exaltation of oneiric flights. The publication of his collected works (*Obra poética 1971–1980*) offers the opportunity of considering the variety of his poetic odyssey.

Justo Jorge Padrón was born in the city of Las Palmas, Grand Canary Island, in 1943. He studied law, philosophy and liberal arts at Barcelona University and later extended his studies in Paris and Stockholm. For seven years he maintained a legal practice until he gave it up to devote himself entirely to literature. To poetry, however, he brings the lawyer's pursuit of the precise word coupled with the wide experience of a translator in dealing with different sensibilities and poetic styles. Padrón lived in Sweden for several years, won a number of prizes for his translations into Spanish of Scandinavian poetry (including the international awards of the Swedish Academy and the National Institute of Norwegian Culture), and, in the words of Academy member Artur Lundkvist, established himself as 'the essential mediator between Nordic and Spanish literatures'.

Justo Jorge's first book, *Los oscuros fuegos* (The Dark Fires, 1971; Second Prize in the Adonais Awards of 1970) is an elegiac farewell to youth and, seemingly, to hope itself. The first and fourth sections of the book are devoted to pondering the passage of time and the lost memories of the past. The paradox of the title refers to the intensity of human experience and the nocturnal pallor of its recollection. These poems are informed with a sense of personal failure, of defeat, but not due to an external cause unless time itself. Part of that defeat, as the poem, 'Today Your Heart Is a Useless Touch', shows, is the result of the poet's own deep-rooted fear of life. Another poet of the 1950s, Angel González, once remarked in an interview that his first book, *Aspero mundo* (Harsh World, 1956) was born from the experience of loneliness and a vague sense of inherited failure. The feeling of failure in Padrón, however, is not so much inherited as metaphysical, a feature of hostile reality itself. Whereas González will use irony and sardonicism to deal with failure and will relate it to his historical-political context, Padrón will search for solace in love, or his imagination will find an outlet in visions of beauty or terror.

Whereas *The Dark Fires* does not have any specifically visionary poems, we are not confronted with a realism evoking past events. The imagery of this first book presages that of the poet's third work, the hallucinatory *Circles of Hell*. Thus in 'A Lasting Faith', the insubstantiality of the poet's identity is driven home by comparing his image to fog just as the poem, 'In the Circular Room', from the later book, will claim that the poet is black smoke. And if the lines, 'My life revolving / In blue mirrors of harmony' remind one of the fresh innocence of Padrón's fourth book, *The Birch Tree in Flames*, it should not be forgotten that mirrors are usually a negative image of man's labyrinthine condition. So the 'faces that pass by' in another text, 'In the Strange City', are referred to as:

> All the grey indifference
> Of mirrors without mercury,
> The encirclement, the slippery void
> You are made to feel by their fates
> Led by the strings of routine.

The leap from faces to mirrors to the void in itself indicates the origin of that hallucinatory style which Padrón later develops more fully in *The Circles of Hell* where mirrors and the abyss are main symbols for man's lost condition.

Nonetheless we should also emphasize that the void is inspired by 'the strings of routine'. The third section of *The Dark Fires* deals largely with the monotony of military life which the poet is forced to endure because of conscription. But it also signals an important theme in Padrón's poetry, the crippling hold of office life that converts human effort into monotonous sameness. In the poem, 'Beneath the Grey-Born Wolf', an empire of sameness demands that men bow down to receive the milk of State, the insipid sustenance of their bureaucratic institutions. No wonder that the poet, in 'A Loyal Endurance', chooses to side with 'the rebels of the night', the students, Bohemians and 'sullen visionaries' that produce in him a permanent sympathy.

The poems of love in the third section of *The Dark Fires* offer an island of tenderness, a moment when love lasts and is enough, but the opening poem, 'First Absence', also prefigures the poet's obsessive fear of loneliness and his search for woman, not only as a place to bury his desires but also a perspective from which to feel oneness with the universe as the poet later expresses in *The Circles of Hell* and especially in *Otesnita*.

Justo Jorge Padrón's second book, *Mar de la noche* (Sea of the Night, 1973; Boscán Award, 1972) is an altogether more disturbing transcendence into a world of uncertainty where hallucinations begin to have the upper hand with respect to reality. The book opens with a fine poem, 'Return', that details the sensations of youth and portrays the poet's youthful musings as a 'watery grove of dreams'. But the same text indicates that life is an implacable passage to that sea of uncertainty which pounds the hopes of man. The most radical use of the sea as a metaphor for man's fragmentation comes in a poem called 'As If You Woke Up in a Strange Country' where a shipwreck leads to the imagined explosion of the body itself in the abysmal pain of waiting for nothingness. The last poems of the book isolate the poet in a nightmare world of visions and guilt from which he cannot escape. In the end the poet is imprisoned by his own fears and is locked in the stasis of a psychological torment where, as he describes in one particular poem, he feels surrounded by eyes that shed no forgiveness.

This self-inflicted torment may be partially owing to what the poet sees in the waters of a river, 'a lonely and incurable desire', 'a taste of burning skin spilling into thirst', and 'a passion created by death / With a radiance more beautiful than life'. Here Padrón reveals an obsessive and romantic yearning that cannot be satisfied by reality. The poems of *Sea of the Night* swing from moments of love that make the poet believe in life to the terrible realization, as he says in another text, that his heart 'sees nothing'. The knowledge of physical love and the emotional harassment when love dies lead the poet on a frenetic search for hope in a context of despair. One of the best metaphysical expressions of this idea occurs in 'Like Someone Springing Up from Autumn' where an allegorical figure brings joy and song to a hopeless family and then departs, leaving the members of the house 'only waiting, waiting for a stranger.'

The ultimate cosmic expression of man's alienation for Padrón is to be found in his fourth and best-known work, *Los circulos del Inferno* (The Circles of Hell, 1976; Fastenrath Award of the Spanish Royal Academy, 1977), a frenetic and visionary attempt to come to grips with the loss of individual identity in a world where love no longer exists. The work is composed of four sections: mutations refer to frightening metamorphoses into a Kafkasque beetle, a tree, a snake and finally stone itself. These nightmarish changes result from an individual existential nausea induced by one's physical and mental being. But from the opening line of the book, 'My mind must be in some strange place', to the last, 'And I am searching in vain', it is clear that the poet's personal anguish stands not only for his isolation but for the defenseless condition of humanity itself. Thus the first poem of the book, 'The Invasion of the Atoms', describes 'A suicidal planet / That burst inside us', and this explosion is imagined as an atomic destruction. Man's individual loathing for himself is projected into nature so that it is impossible to tell whether he is destroyed from within or from without. In the final poem of the volume Padrón offers a labyrinthine vision of death itself as the poet with images of amputation, feels he is sinking into the darkness of what is past, there where

> The dead keep falling from rivers and tombs,
> From nights and crimes and forgotten centuries,
> Revolving towers of eyes and rigid faces
> Like columns, an icy museum
> Of gestures, a cloudy vapour among veins of stone . . .

One is reminded of the 'vertical river of the dead' in Pablo Neruda's poem, 'Soló la muerte' ('Only Death'), but instead of death being a journey upstream, Padrón imagines it as an irreversible descent into the depths of an ocean. Towards the end of this poem, the island poet gives a clue to what may be the real hell for him when he refers to 'no noise, no sign, / No voice, no silence'. The nether world where one has neither the clarity of sound nor the definitiveness of silence, not even a place to nurture a voice — this is where humanity finds its torment. Justo Jorge pointedly chose this title for an earlier anthology of his work, *Ningún ruido, ningún silencio* (No Noise, No Silence, 1978).

The third section of *The Circles of Hell* presents a somewhat more realistic version than the others of 'Hell on Earth'. The 'First Absence' poem of *The Dark Fires* now becomes a delirious image of hate and hurt in the poem, 'Madness'. A terrible loneliness informs this part of the book, a sense, as one text says, that man's dignity is just a 'pale wet scrap of paper'. But if extreme despair leads to the contemplation of suicide in which man disintegrates in terms of natural imagery, the will to survive is offered as the one spur to lead us on.

Not all the poems of Padrón's third book are bleak. Two fine texts render a portrait of sensual woman with her 'shiver of water and silk' and, significantly, 'The Dream of Returning to Childhood' and 'The Eyes of the Night' describe two things that can never be stolen from the poet: the magic of infancy and the sense of the house as an eternal home. But the last section, confirming Nobel Laureate Vicente Aleixandre's opinion of the work as 'an imprisoning symbol of man's fate', renders the chasms in the mirror of the self as well as a Gothically allegorical placement of man, with his terrors and uncertainty, in a tunnel full of spiders.

Perhaps the only possible answer to a book as extreme as *The Circles of Hell* is one like *The Birch Tree in Flames* (*El abedul en llamas*, 1978). In this austere idyll amidst the natural setting of Scandinavia, Padrón heals the wounded spirit of his previous work while he develops, in brief poems, little vignettes of nature, a fresh facet of his poetic sensibility. There is an occasional note of gloom — the last verse of the book even refers to a 'dark impulse of hate or death' — but if the poet is one who has to accept the unlucky fate of 'the failure and the flame', he also practices 'The diaphanous craft / Of a minute art.' Padrón turns his precision of word on various aspects of the elements, water, sea, birch tree, the flora and fauna of brisk, northern summers, and from them, extracts brief sensations of beauty.

The spiritual goal of the book is the poet's search for 'renunciation and light', perhaps partially a retreat from the darker regions of himself but also a desire to find permanence in the ephemeral changes of the seasons. Light is one of the main images throughout and on different occasions finds its metaphorical partner in an aura, dragonflies, an eagle or stars. The astral meets the particular to allow the rebirth and song of stillness. The two sections of *The Birch Tree in Flames*, 'The Terrestrial Seasons' and 'Leaves of Memory', evoke a search for human harmony in the features of a landscape and describe the different leaves of experience from the tree of one man's life: the memories of an old woman, of previous loves, of contrasting lands and lasting friendships. Two poems from the latter part of the book linger in the mind: a tribute to Mexican poet Octavio Paz and a haunting description of the northern lights. Both illustrate the way Padrón's poems are, as he states in his introduction to his collected works, 'the fruit of vehement intuitions'. While *The Birch Tree in Flames* is a quieter, more harmonious work than *The Circles of Hell*, it combines a sharp eye for detail with the dreamlike, visionary and occasionally, cosmogonic perspective which is perhaps Padrón's most distinctive contribution to the young poetry from Spain. Thus Octavio Paz is conceived of as a tamer of words, of those 'Strange animals crossing from mystery / To silence, discovering its imprisoned blood.' In 'Aurora Borealis in Iceland', the description of this natural phenomenon merges with a delirious creation: 'Eyes, icy and intense, loomed up in the mist / Music staffs, sails, flags, /Embers and flowers of the locked light / Cruising on the heights . . . '

Otesnita, Justo Jorge Padrón's brief fifth book, portrays in the two phases of its diptych the ecstatic emotion of an ode and the desolate loss of an elegy. It describes not merely a fleeting love affair but the distance between stellar desire and the reality of earthly disappointment. In this respect, it presents the clearest example of the two predominant moods in Padrón's poetry: the sense of delight and enthrallment, and the corrosion of despair.

Otesnita is the name invented by the poet to designate the woman and the impossible aura of tenderness and natural beauty which he discovers in her. On the one hand, the poet wants to so deny his individuality that he can become part of her 'startled light' and envision her as a 'unique, blue planet', a telluric goal; on the other, he has presentiments of the brevity of their love: 'after our fire / Only fear and ashes will remain . . . ' The ambivalence of desire, the quest for the eternal in ephemerality of feeling, leads to the inevitable disappointment and the pain of emptiness, but the description of the poet's living injury in terms of a natural setting is one of the distinctive and poignant features of the book. The flight of a seagull halting in the air is transformed into 'a tear searching for a face'.

His next volumes were *La visita de mar* (The Sea's Visit),

and *Los Dones de la Tierra* (Gifts of the Earth). 'The Sea's Visit' has three sections: 'The Garden of the Sun', 'The Losing Years', and 'The Dreams of Death', which correspond with day, dusk and night. The sense of wonder at nature is especially acute in the poems of the first part which range from a description of the rooster's clarion call to the poet's immersion in the sea of thought that 'gives names to the hostile transparence' of a blank page. It also includes a visit of Neptune in all his briny splendour and a poem on the poet as a magician who enlists the blackbird's song.

The second section on dusk details the awakening of fear and doubt in man. One poem, 'Night in the Cry', offers a fine example of what Spanish Poet Carlos Bousoño calls the 'proliferating image' as used in his book, *Las monedas contra la losa* (The Coins Against the Counter, 1973). In this trope, the central ideal of the poem is embodied in a single image that spurs the imagination throughout the rest of the poem. Padrón achieves this effect with a new concision.

The final section of *The Sea's Visit*, Night, responds to the moment of man's awareness that there is no way out and that death is the final solution. The poems extend from an interpretation of stone to the final poem of the volume, an apocalyptic vision of the end as an atomic rain that recalls 'The Invasion of the Atoms' from *The Circles of Hell*. The colour blue, a note of freedom, appears often in *The Sea's Visit*. Perhaps it is in this volume that he gives freest rein to the gamut of his moods in the fitful and concise drama of his poetic journey.

These contrasts can be appreciated in the basic elements of the work. On the one hand, the sea is largely a positive force embellished with metaphors from architecture, flora and fauna. 'The Red Rose', for example, compares the flower to Venus emerging from the sea's petals. It helps, too, to know that this particular poem in the original was dedicated to the poet's mother, hence an allegorical reading is intended. On the other hand, where the sea ends in 'Deep Waters', the poet finds himself, in the night of life, rowing eternally in the deep waters of a melancholy consciousness.

Another element, the poetic word, begins dressing life with vitality, but it also gradually strips its creator to the condition of a prisoner, leaving him its poison. If Padrón often lives the beings of predatory animals, he knows he is stalked by time. The individual's disappearance becomes a collective nuclear holocaust where Italian poet Cesare Pavese's notion that death will come and have your eyes, is transformed into corrosive tears from the heavens.

Little wonder, then, that the brief book that follows, *Los dones de la tierra* (The Gifts of Earth), seeks relief from personal concerns in lyric descriptions of the four basic elements. If Neruda and Aleixandre also dealt with elemental things, Padrón now describes the human alliance with substances that were, for pre-Socratic philosophers, the origin of life, and they serve to join the familiar with the mysterious, reminding us of 'a God' that is within and without.

Padrón's final book to date, *Sólo muere la mano que te escribe* (Only the Hand That Writes You Dies, in press), includes five sections: 'Heard Faces', 'The Workshop of Writing', 'Love or its Chimera', 'The Pebbles of Coldness' and 'Notebook of Mount Lentiscal'. It is perhaps the poet's most metaphysical work as it goes beyond the finality of death in the previous book to deal with the cosmic as a place where the dead retrench and insinuate the subsoil of our existence. His preoccupation with the source of his writing is extended and deepened. His island home again makes the memory speak. And the love poems, with their sensual and often delirious imagery, are among the most interesting that he has written, testimonies of searching, failure and self-recognition. The dot that disappears in an earlier poem, 'The Boy and the Stone', again disappears in the 'Fable of Two Castaways', the death of childhood now the death of a romance. It is significant that the book opens with a poem that serves as a prologue, 'The Hand That Writes You'. Poetry is embodied in a beautiful woman and the poet's attempt to make her last.

Free verse in Spanish, especially in Spain, is not free, and most poets, as well as Padrón, write in hendecasyllabic lines, varying these with others of seven, nine and fourteen syllables, for the eleven-syllable line has something like the tradition and musicality of the iambic pentameter in English poetry, and the other lines maintain the rhythm but offer dramatic variety. Part of Padrón's art is his dedication to the music of his verses. Regarding the resources of his language, Swedish poet Artur Lundkvist spoke of *The Circles of Hell* as one of the most important books of the new European poetry, particularly for its 'original, visionary and metaphorical ability'. The recent awarding to Padrón of the European Literature Prize in Yugoslavia is a confirmation of that judgement. Perhaps one proof may be in the pages that follow.

Louis Bourne
Madrid
October, 1987

from
The Dark Fires
Los oscuros fuegos
(1971)

A LOYAL ENDURANCE

From insomnia's disturbing tunnel
I heard the trains' long and distant whistle
And the rain's zigzag growing in the wind.
Eyes that in that room's
Black void sought
Useless protection —
Knew the night's violent call.
Hoarse humming of engines,
Drunken voices, miaowing of cats on heat,
Scratched the sleeping city's
Intermittent silence.

Like fog,
On slow, distant steps
My lonely image climbed.
Lost streets — rough paths
In other lands to which I was led
By chance — assumed their former shape,
Their uncontrollable splendour.
Clocks from other hours
Pointed to the dark fires
Of the past. There were
The students, the songs
Of dawn, the Bohemians'
Joyful wine,
The unfading oratory
Of sullen visionaries,
And the smoke and the women
As though still waiting for me.

I don't know if, knowing them,
Their joy or their loneliness
Were the same in me.
But since then a strange love
With a symbol's stubborn power
Still links me to those nameless
Rebels of the night
Who rally behind the banners
Of a loyal endurance.

LOOKING BACKWARD

Remembrance comes to us
When we hide behind wet windowpanes
An absent face, and then, confused
In memory, lies the city
We contemplate in our calm.
Slowly what made us sad
Looms up like the trail of smoke
In a feeble passing.
In the tumult of the past
We eagerly touch
A hope that might save us;
And so, the hostile frontiers of the present
Erased, without our awareness
A lukewarm feeling invites us to fathom
The warm hours we lived.
A more intense sparkling,
A questioning voice,
Pours out for us the naked reality.
Immune through habit
We reject the luminous image
Of that never-repeated past
To return sorrowfully
To that other world of ashes
Which little by little we went on destroying
With the length of our indifference.

AS ON THE FIRST DAY

Slowly you keep sewing
The dress in the machine,
Your daughter's dreams.
Fabric and the light
Braided together in your hands.
I watch you and begin to feel a blood
Thrill. I am speaking
To you without moving
My lips,
As though words didn't exist.

It's a lighted silence
We listen to between our white
Walls. The machine goes on
Backstitching dreams;
Hope is clothed
In a little girl's outfit.
Hardly a hint
Of a glance and we find ourselves
As on the first day.
Love lasts. And it's enough.

IF JUST ONCE

If just once you'd show me
How you love me, I'd believe
More in life. Like wheat
Seed, I'd scatter myself from your faith to earth.
How lovely the yearning to burn out
In the world's fire, fused in its love,
Becoming matter and dreams.
But he who believes this is transformed
Into the brief, real image
Of a space pondered with all the beauty
Of a god enjoying and igniting what he touches.

The heart revives
When singing in the limits of the lover,
When born budding in her light,
And prefers death before exodus,
Because to leave — stone said so before — is to die,
To fertilize forgetting.

FIRST ABSENCE

After the long trip
I come back home, as on so many occasions,
To you who wait for me
With your love and its candles lit
On the set table.
So I dreamed, new and recurring,
The foreseen encounter.
And the wind pushed me
And the rain increased my desires.
I opened the door
And a thick breath
Like darkness
Struck me in the face.
Only a cold silence waited,
The furniture huddled together,
Smelling of no one.
The wind whispered
Among the autumn pines . . .
But I am not resigned,
I deny loneliness
And I invent you in the house as you were then.
I light up this room
Where you were sewing
And you come back from the depths of memory.
Till suddenly
I see on your chair a dress
Left behind, I caress it
As though it were lived by you,
And my hands find themselves
Empty in the air.
I love and look for your things
And the rain continues,
And despair comes in all alone
On the first night of your absence.

THE LIGHT OF EVERY AFTERNOON

In the old armchair,
After the blind bustle of this day,
The slow hours of silence come to me.
The warm words have already gone
On the dark wind of absence.
Bright, former voices
Reach me from memory:
My life revolving
In blue mirrors of harmony.
The joyful house
Lured me to its fresh shade.

But I don't know if time
Suddenly darkens my eyes
Or if my skin no longer recalls the deep
Vitality. I only remain
In the orphanhood of an instant,
Thinking of you, thinking
Of the shadowy years that descend
Every afternoon in the light
Of this final, faithful loneliness.

ON THESE OLD HILLS

On these old hills,
Beside many other men,
They force me to learn
On the cutting edge of cold and loathing,
Obeying, always obeying
The anonymous cry of command.
There, in the background, the sea,
The sea always surrounding us
With its distant and relentless steel.
Later, in the rhythmic
Breathing of bodies
Sunk in the sordid dereliction
Of sweat and effort,
The wounding and desolate night falls,
And the weariness of each one
Climbs heavily towards the canvas
Covering our absurd apprenticeship
Day after day.

FRIGHTENED SHADOWS

The bugle
Like a cold fist
Deprives us of sleep.
Lean profiles
Of fear stand out
In dawn's wavering light.
And the frightened shadows
Run, run,
To the ordered assembly.
Bitter faces
Of silence fall into
Dark ranks.
And no voice
Breaks the wind's thread,
Only a clattering of plates,
Of pots, lends
Its sorrowful sound to a day
That broke without horizons.

BENEATH THE GREY-BROWN WOLF

Prisoner in the indifference of these walls,
And disillusioned
In the midst of files and orders
Belonging to men who never wanted to bow down
Beneath the grey-brown wolf,
I view my escaping youth
Tied to fear,
The joyful, bright fiesta
Of this day blazing without my being able
To squeeze it, drink it in the middle of the street
As though it were a piece of fruit,
I . . . free and different like all the rest.

THE DARK HOURS

The dark hours squandered
With the grim vehemence of what no longer returns,
You watch how dawn now lights up
Your defeat, your longing to find
Another cause to survive you.
And once more you review,
Like a deck's
Fast cards, the night's rough places,
Signs and remains. In rowdy bars
You've rejected stray hands
And the offer of greedy lips,
And, intermittently, in the sea's
Nearby murmur, you make out the meaningless
Voices spilling in their barren game
Of speaking and not being.

Behind, like a useless burden, remain
The unhelpful experiences
Leaving only their aftertaste of want.
With the same anxiety, the squalid city
Wakes up long, lonely streets.
You look at the dawning light,
A balcony's sudden gleaming,
Someone's astonished face,
Harsh new environs that show
Roads offering you
A possible return,
Maybe the truest and most foreseen.
The stubborn passion for life
Without limits involves that hope,
And you wear a vanquished smile, for now
Prompt memory remembers and denies.

You keep on down the street,
Your back to the accompanying light,
Tripping over scruffy dogs that get up early,
Hearing their wild racket,
And the roosters' electric blast
Shattering morning.
And you arrive, and fearfully open
The door you know,
And suddenly you meet your past,
The familiar odour of all that made you one.
Hesitating, you watch yourself
In a mirror's cruel surface

11

And hate him grimacing
From his sad depths
To cheer your return again.
You go stealthily into
The bedroom. Naked and old, you hug
Your warm, frightened body
While you're seized by an unquenchable dream.

IN THE STRANGE CITY

In the dark north's strange city,
The one with long bridges and canals,
In underground trains, hounded
By cold and solitude,
You go on, bitter foreigner,
Like a shadow, looking for yourself.

You notice impenetrable expressions
Of faces passing by,
All the grey indifference
Of mirrors without mercury,
The siege, the slippery void
You are made to feel by their fates
Led by threads of routine.

On this dazzling transit, decors
And estranged lives come one after another,
Scenes and silences
That will never merge.
And you, perhaps unlike them all,
Search for a gaze to halt
Your uncertain journey, a smile
To give back your lost image:
Passion for life.

TODAY YOUR HEART
IS A USELESS TOUCH

With the surety of someone waiting for nothing
You open — in no hurry — the old gate
And listen to the sluggish
Steps, that don't seem yours,
On the grey stairway.
No voice offers you its warmth,
And you walk in darkness. Nothing
Takes you to your corner, not even music,
Nor the old poets, nor are the worn
Love letters company for you.
Tonight
Through your memory pass the lost
Names that at other times
Gave deep credence to your youth.
The wind's whisper arrives,
Your life's tedious emptiness,
And you recognize yourself in it,
For you love him who was
And sense the absence
Of your best days.
Today your heart is a useless touch,
You know it and cannot delude yourself.
Still you let memory, unafraid,
Run off with all you loved,
Everything you lost on this barren earth:
That blind fear of life which maybe
You always had: your failure.
But nothing matters to you now, and you gaze
Through the window at the most tenacious tree,
Fill your glass and think:
This is the legacy of a man alone.

from
Sea of the Night
Mar de la noche
(1973)

RETURN

The first light that broke in my life
Was the warm kingdom of odours.

I never let the darkness come
To sow fear in me.
I clung to the unmistakable wool
Of my charger made of rag,
To the lush white balls of fresh cork,
To my grandfather's old
Books that, under the pillow,
Brought me the pollen
Of a world foreseen.

Later I knew the sea,
Its big blue embrace splitting my senses,
Filling my fearless childhood
With quivering presences.
In the first classrooms
I fondled the green maps. Blackboards of black smoke
And winged desks carried me off
To the watery grove of dreams.

There, the motionless inkpot stared at me
With its black eye and courteous bowler,
And the box of pencils
Made joy awake to new colours.

And what a delight the ball at playtime,
A frolicking planet for our nimble feet,
Leaving between our hands
Its tight feel of drum and watermelon
And of shoe-shops tanned by the wind.

Then that night so different from all others:
The weightless walk beneath the summer pines
And a breeze irresistibly laying bare
The wild aromas.
Under the lurking leaves we stretched out
Making the dry pine needles tremble
And, for the first time, the body of love.
What headiness,
What a strange choking blaze
For all the senses. And I kept forever
Those enfolding odours that still burn me
Like a virgin baptism with earth.

And then, faster and faster, life
Carrying me off swirling by perfumes and bodies,
Rooms and words, mists,
Tunnels, good-byes, dawns, silences,
Which little by little kept stripping me
Of all love and the soaring confidence I felt.

Now that everything has gone, again,
Tired, longing,
I start to walk.
In this room full of worlds,
These books from all ages
Bring to me once more
The lost aroma of woodlands and people,
Filling my life and distance
With the tenderness of this beloved kingdom
Fragrantly rising
From the restive pulse of paper.

IN THE WATER

When I go back to the old bridge,
I gaze at the city fading
In the slow memories of afternoon.
The image of your body quivering
Drifts by in sad, troubled waters.
Dark eddies summon me
To their mirror's depth.
They speak to me of a sudden vertigo,
Of a passion created by death
With a radiance lovelier than life.
All is the air's scent and strange power,
Floating forests in the river's
Rainbow light, youthfulness of bodies,
A taste of burning skin spilling into thirst . . .
The water flows, and under it
A lonely, incurable desire.

A NEVER-REPEATED GIFT

After rewalking familiar roads
And slowly remembering again
With no illusions, as if you couldn't
Return to the motionless mass of what was lived,
And were not able to take a single step, I gaze
Through this autumn's sandy fires,
And suddenly tremble.

Lucid and taciturn,
Hearing a soft wind among the trees,
I muse on new life
Springing up around me.
Young lovers walk by, borne
By a vehemence aching in my memory,
And children still playing,
Lifting their eyes to the clear vision
Of a world now lost.
I raise my glass touched by the light
Of this peaceful afternoon,
And I toast life
Passing like a never-repeated gift.

I CROSS THE NIGHTS

I look for your liquid eyes
In a new day's dawning.
Rain and my dereliction
Have brought me to these streets,
To these bars without you where night
Still hides. My eyes
Look for you as though they could not
Understand the past.
Now that vast quicksands tremble in my body
And hope is gutted by the endless wind,
I feel the cold beat against trees and stones,
And, devastated, I called you like a blind dog.
Through long avenues I keep wandering from you,
Through strange places where you never were;
I look for you and write you words growing lost
Along canals and sidewalks,
And with your name I wound this tired wind.
Nothing has remained since you went,
And you are no longer like a shower of gold
Lending light and fire to my naked blood.
Straying in lingering daybreaks,
I cross the nights like dead water
Tattooed with an invisible scar.

WHERE LIPS MEET

With the light's drunken
Murmur, at the strange place
Where lips meet,
The transparent glow
Of two splendid bodies.

From this sheer union,
Fire of waves and hands,
Tongues, thighs and hips
Breathe the frenzy,
Destruction and happiness
Of one unanimous body.

Between agony and jubilation,
With the world's private
Astonishment in your arms,
You cut through the speed of desire,
Its distances disturbing
Chance, and there, wrapped
In that matchless radiance of love
So often sought,
You begin the surprise
Of believing in life.

IN IDLE WHISTLING

The heart with sad strings
Dreams, rings shrilly
In the grove's most hidden
Nooks or in my saddest
Boot, pierced through
With the eyes and mouths of utter desolation.
It's the impossible, diving
And desolate music
Dragging me on, driving me
Toward the brush, toward the lost
Flight of leaves
Erasing me in the afternoon's fallen light.
There, an idle whistling
Guiding my steps
Through a dark confine
Of clothes drenched with apathy and tears,
Strangely mingles
With the time lived through, half-dreamed,
Lost and barrenly searched for
In this heart seeing nothing.

THE BURNING WAVE
SWEEPS YOU ALONG

Meanness and slander,
And their bastard merchants
Spread through all your memory
Like a curse.
Muffled, the violent fist of days
Explodes in your blood with every blow.
You arrive home, worn out with the somber stench
Of defeat, but your look
In its factious rebellion
Swears you've still not lost.

The burning wave sweeps you along
Through the small shadowy passage.
Without realizing it,
You start setting fire to the walls,
The books, even the obedient air of home,
And you bring down everything with your dark look.
Huge sticky eyes hang from the doorways,
Twisted tongues smudge
Peaceful paintings and mirrors,
And shelves and furniture topple
Before your desolate steps.
All the scum of the world stains your bed,
Contaminating everything you loved with your presence,
And at last you find yourself and rush downstairs,
Before even your house
Stops being the one refuge
Against death.

THE DEFEATED MAN

In the depth of a cup of coffee
He recognizes his face,
The lost smile
That never seemed to age.
The steam emerges from its blackness,
Drapes from the gloomy walls of winter.
Alone. Finally alone,
He understands so much struggle,
So much useless comforting word,
So man can defend himself from fear.
He smiles because it's pleasant to recall
How life was a joyful ignorance:
The continual hope of desire.

But the lesson could not be salvaged.
And now with the locked limits of the present,
Far from dreams
Or drunken moments,
He gazes at his face cloudily reflected
In the seething silt of coffee
And in its mirror he senses
The pulse of time,
The whisper of words dying away,
And in the silence he learns to grasp
Acceptance of the world,
For he knows that life
Is just a brief foreboding
Of death and nothingness.

IN THIS DARKNESS

Maj-Gun's breasts
Like two sunflowers unfolding in the night.
Of Janine, the feline curve
Rolling always in unexpected flights.
The sensitive purring
Of Concha the Cuban
Like a warm, spilling kiss.
Ingrid's strange beating, bell-like
And solemn, and Marion with her mouth
Biting and submissive.

These were the bright cloudy bodies
I knew. Those beds
Still gleam, throb,
Spreading their seminal scent
Throughout memory.
                              Now
They are all one in the imagination,
One in my frailty,
Near a point rising up
Over this darkness
Like a lost cry in the void.

WITH THE SAME MADNESS

It could be said the love that made us one
Avenges each day
By keeping us together.
Our drunken gazing
So full of passion and enhancing sound
Has given way to a jarring dialogue
In which words
Like creepers or ignited stones
Slam our eyes. Sometimes a song
From the first days or a poignant shadow
Remains in our presence,
And it's one of us who blurts out
The shameless irony, the fierce recollection,
The buried anger.
Blind and relentless is our faithful destruction,
And to it we set ourselves with the same vehemence
With which we began to love,
With the same keenness and tact,
The same madness
Of this common trick cutting off our escape.

LIKE SOMEONE
SPRINGING UP FROM AUTUMN

'Are you here?'
'We're all dead,' I replied gloomily.
And without paying us the slightest attention,
He came in like one more member
Of the house.
He arrived like someone springing up from autumn,
From a sorrow,
Maybe even further away, from a forgotten dream.
And he unloaded his bundle of joy
In the grim corners.
He smoothed down his weary hair
Of rain and winds.
He sat down beside us
And lived all the aromas
Of the room. He gave us
His simple heart,
Lit up the songs, now lost,
From water and fires.
He urged us to go on,
Not to suffer that bitter death,
And he spread out before us
The roads that lead to life.
He embraced us in the end one by one,
And a powerful light suffused our lips.
With watery eyes,
We accompanied him to the horizon.
We asked him for a last word:
'What name can we remember you by?'
The voice, almost smoke,
Scarcely reached us.
And since then our lives
Have been only waiting, waiting for a stranger.

THE SLEEPER

Disturbing odours from scattered vases
Awake the night's supremacy.
You keep watch,
And while all are asleep
You quietly reread a book
On the old wisdom of living.
With clasping love, you now bear it off to sleep.
Through the long corridor,
The grim shadows created by the light
Go back to their kingdom of blackness.
Familiar sheets
Welcome you with their warm rustling,
And their scent of protected childhood,
Innocent, forgotten gestures, kisses
Of a rite faithful to the statuette
That ruled over your good sleep,
And now, indifferent,
Yawns at its lost domain of fears;
And the damp hallways return,
The dirty classrooms of the school
And that bitter cassocked voice
With its dark power.

You smile from the distance
Of that forgotten time,
Gloomily confused.
And you see all the tenderness
Of your daily clothes,
Their living company keeping
Your warmth on the chair.
You blind the light. Silence grows
In the shuddering space.
Faint gleams from stars
Reflect climbing white eyes;
Branches of huge trees
Extend a shadowy silhouette;
Leaves restive as lips, fingers
Or startled birds
Cover the room,
And the wind shakes them
On the walls. Deep uncertainty swells,
And it's a dark sea,
Uncontrollable, flooding you
And overwhelming the half-light of the house.

There in the tremulous room in the back,
Is he still living?
And your only doubt was sullen cruelty.
A broad plain of absence then shrouds
Life completely,
Your narrow fear weeps,
Gasps in the pillow,
Searching for sleep, its swift forgetting.
Through your memory cross,
Like a flag
Burning in the wind,
The last shared moments,
His befriending hand, the kindness, the haven,
The world's measure in his word.
Yet fear and haste
Suddenly yank at the sheets,
And you slip secretly
Along the sombre passage.
There, in the family bedroom,
My father sleeps
And a child sits down in the corner nearest him,
Listens to life pulse in each object
With its glad song of momentary truth,
And as on other forgotten nights
Of tenderness and quiet,
The dream comes to rest in his smile.

BEAUTY

No one could have known her strange life.
A traveller of mists and snow,
In her uneasy eyes she gathered
Mystery, light and sorrow.

She walked along sunny streets
Before the wonder of violent men
Who never understood her.

Though they craved her
In an urge for fruitless possession,
She strolled nearby, inaccessible,
Before the dread of all.

One day during their reckless fighting
She crossed the tavern threshold
All morning light.
They were speechless. Even the glasses
Held the silence of respect.
She would offer herself — in return for peace.

She started to undress
And cries of misery
Opened the doors. All escaped.

Lovely — she was nude.

IT'S THE DAY I FEAR

I never felt afraid of night
When I calmly crossed still avenues
Beneath the quiet snapping of trees
In the soft, disturbing darkness.
Nor was I frightened by furtive fingernails
Of rain or wind
Against the clouded windowpanes of dark.
Nor did I find hostility
In whores, tramps or warm-hearted drunks,
Merely companions of nights that sank away.
And I always found my room waiting
At the end of early morning intensities.

It's the day I fear:
Sticky jungle of offices and machines,
Clocks and orders, where hybrid notaries
And orphan clerks grow, grow,
Till they hide even the blind day's sun.

Sickening buses go by, full of mirrors,
Smokey faces revolve, condemned
To go up and down unending streets,
Squalid lifts, corridors, passageways
And lost factories where light doesn't exist
And we're forgotten by love,
Where death, not giving us time,
Welcomes us in trumph.

It's the day I fear.

RINGED BY EYES

In the quivering by which your eyes at night
Read sheets of paper managing
to exist, fear blindly shines.

That fear, relentless and corroding,
Climbing walls and dreams,
Bearing buried, violent
Deaths that still seem to wait
Lurking behind each window.

A motionless air envelops the walls
Of the room. The clock's hand
Strikes the invisible sleepers.
Behind the crystals of the mist: mouths,
Footsteps of a whispering human river
Rising in waves along the naked,
Smoking folds of the sheets.

It's a silent crowd,
Tense and accusing, remaining
In compact circles of the air.
They are eyes, countless eyes pondering
Your life's misery and light.

With a criminal's anguished keenness,
You see the room has been reduced
To the strict limits of a niche
Interred in time. Without a captive
Moon or star-strewn waters,
Without the sea of the night or the trees'
Distant voices, there,
There you stay, ringed by eyes
That cannot forgive or forget.

from
The Circles of Hell
Los círculos del infierno
(1976)

THE INVASION OF THE ATOMS

My mind must be in some strange place,
Far away from this voice that's not mine.
This voice not even the wind can spread
Is lost memories gathered
In a nervous whisper, in a frail moan
From many other men who have already died;
They are cells of life, thoughts scattered
By the supreme explosion of the light.
An instant that has lived for centuries;
Centuries, just that one instant.
We can remember it only with effort.

It was a shrieking mirror,
A suicidal planet
That burst inside us
And spilled out the sudden madness
Of the light, all fire's fire,
The single cry of every stroke of lightning
That seemed to lift earth's
Loathsome depths into the air.
We were overwhelmed by the black vibration from the abyss,
The cobalt's blinding stain
Erasing colours, corroding plains,
Crumpling buildings like dirty papers,
Drying up flowers, clouds, blinding feathers, seas.
With a metallic din, it flattened mountain ranges
And soaked through children's sleeping pores.

Everything was pierced by its destructive eye
And life and earth eaten to the core,
And water never again became water
And air never air any more.
Everything was bereft of soul and quiet sound.
Everything broken, lost in itself, stark,
Frozen forever in the snapshot
Of desolation and death.
It was time out-of-joint, and meaning,
Enraged mutation, glittering leprosy,
Man's history utterly destroyed.

We are ashes among the shadows,
A wisp of smoke that chance has barely drawn together,
A trace of man in atoms broken up,
Something that, in its slipping, is imbued
With the liquid substances of slime,
And a word or warning for no one ever again.

STENCH

A stench awakes him,
And he can see nothing.
The shadow never changes,
No gradation or nuance in the blackness,
A sewer in the depths of the onyx,
The supreme hollow, the helplessness.

He starts to grope in the unending denseness.
He can only make out the muffled squelching
Of footsteps through the mire.

The anguish is
Like lethal shadow, like a slow acid on the skin.

Distant gusts of wind pursue him,
Shoving him in hostile directions, dragging him along.
Blindly he keeps advancing, tearing the darkness
With the seething weight behind him.

He reels in the dizziness. His only idea is to flee,
Escape from those blind surroundings.

He walks steadily faster, listening to
The furious gasping, the thick death rattles
From thousands of creatures or perhaps from a huge
Gill with its broken breathing.

He falls, trips, races
Deliriously toward nowhere.

That wind with wings of a giant raven
Wounds him from every corner
With the dread of the unknown.

His hands strike, sink into a wet mass.
He remains motionless as the silence.

His astonished touch shows him
A grim surface.
Unable to go forward, to take one step,
He keeps hearing icy quivers that seek him out.

Trembling, he now lifts his hand
And feels and slides it
Over that taut substance,
Long and retractile.

By its breathing
And the dark snapping of the wings
He learns of the presence of a being his own size.

Desperately he runs, burning himself
In the filth.
And when he reaches the last limit of pain,
The complete disintegration of fear,
He feels his long, exhausted legs.

But his hands touch two long feelers,
And below, two wings outspread.

There once more were
The convulsive antennae,
The wings, the cold, sticky chest:
His tiny body.

THAT LEAFY WEIGHT

I listened to a rocking of oars in my body
As though they were swinging the morning sun.
A din of silver bells in the hollows of the air.
A warm gust, a crackling sound swaying.
I could not feel my arms. They had turned
Into lanky members that sought the light.
The wind shook me, made me rustle
Like a trembling bird tied to earth
That could no longer get loose and fly away.
What could be my shape? Over my skin
There was a foul migration, a tiny exodus
Of short light legs. It was a waving
Wet procession of trembling needles
Like flood water bearing smoke and pebbles.
On another of my sides, a sudden touch
Of beak, talons and nails. I felt the wind, the sun,
The invisible seething of the growing earth,
And I tried to free myself from that leafy weight.
My body rang softly with a wavering music,
With mystery and no wrath, motionless in the earth,
Condemned to exist, to be part of time,
And to wait, wait, for the lightning bolt, the fire and the axe.

AUTOPHAGY

I woke up stretched out in a room
Covered with gleaming mirrors.
In that sealed-off enclosure, the slow growth
Of my neck reflected sharply.
And it grew and grew, gradually
Setting my eyes farther away from my trunk.
That shudder of terror
Went on multiplying along ceilings and walls
And pursued me in scarcely any space.

The shriek rebounded between those walls
Of quicksilver and ice, and my skin stretched,
Reducing my arms and legs
To stumps, fins, to finish up as
Only a glittering, scaly surface.
As my body suddenly swayed
Like a thick cable, I saw two powerful eyes
Whose muddy thirst scanned me
From every corner of each mirror.
I went on listening to the hiss of slithering spite,
And the bristling head wheeled on itself
And began swallowing me by swallowing itself.

AN ENDLESS STILLNESS

The whispering grove of trees remained behind,
The dream amidst the light and among the birds,
The living love and the lush growth of friendship.
And the gilded clattering chariot of ambition
And triumph rolled by,
Vanity's haughty fever
And the useless day's work
In the grey galley of routine.
Even that enormous zeal
For reconciling life in the word
Was gradually left behind as well,
And memory and extinct desire
Returned to their Cambrian waters.

The fog went on shrouding a silent time.

Now I hardly feel
The light's faint persistence,
And a strange fatigue,
And a powerful weight,
And an endless stillness
Tell me more than any words can say:
Now I am stone.

IF GOD GREW TIRED OF US

If God grew tired of us,
If God hated us,
He'd start changing us slowly,
Put a leprosy of time on our skins,
Sicken our sensibilities
And make the thirst and anguish
Of memory unending;
And at our side, mirrors,
A multitude of mirrors,
So that day and night
Our losses, unrestrained, would be reflected.
We would feel unseen blows falling
From inside us and from the farthest distances as well.
And we would be locked in sunken confines
And in sordid jobs
Which would go on reducing us to shadow.
To prevent our loving,
He would pour into us ambition,
Envy, violence, lust, hate . . .
This poison would keep rotting away our souls.
From them maimed limbs and spite would spring up,
Countless vices.
And then when, shouting, we'd beg for
Death, he would inspire in the most wary
The merciful custom of prolonging
Our shouts till the limits of terror or insanity.
If this God grew tired of us,
And if this God, so just, hated us,
We'd be the mean
And the shrivelled breed, awkward, blind and suicidal,
Debased and criminal, damned,
Which is the human race.

THE CITY OF DEATH

Here is the city that nightmares
Could never see.

Drawn on a canvas of water,
It looms up floating in the mists.

Dwellings of black space, broken
Beams violently pounding
A wall, a dead world.

Rubble, ruins scattered by the wind,
Rags emerging in the emptiness.
Dried blood, traces that one day were life.

Charred hills,
Skeletons of rotten trees
With that desolate stiffness
Of drowned hands beneath the cracks in the ice.

I lift up my eyes, I see the vastness,
And stars do not exist, nor the blue.
The air is tense with waiting
To be parted by a word.

I am searching in vain for life,
The radiance of roving water,
The leafy fragrance of the trees,
The light, the voice of man.

But all is desert.
Now there is no exit from this labyrinth.
The earth's future image
Is the mirror of this hell.

IN THE CIRCULAR ROOM

In the midst of the circular room,
Through the dense all-embracing dark,
I begin to see on the metallic screen
The scenes, the sweetest and most awful events
That shaped my life. There truth
Appears, the mistakes of my road intensely lived,
As well as the people who walked into my history.
They are silent witnesses,
Time no longer exists. It's a ravaged wind.
I know that only they and a handful of images
Are what remains of my world.

I want to leave this settled lie behind,
This trap, stops the voices,
This welling up of images
In which my time goes on wasting away.
No one, no one listens. Intermittent flashes
Light up the crowded faces.
And I identify them. One by one I speak to them,
Beg them for a love I could never give,
And I search in their eyes for a spark of light.
They are blurred statues
Without the parody of the slightest gesture.
I bring my arms and lips close,
But their suits, their fine hair,
Dissolve into smoke, into stampeding shadows.
I go on searching for a hand, a word
That might show me the door to flight.
Like a Midas of smoke I go on converting everything
Into shadows. The sea does not exist, nor the plains,
Nor the birds, nor laughter, nor even tears.
Nor the statues.
The giant circular room is one total
Mass of smoke. I slowly melt into the anonymous.
I shall not live in death. Now I am black smoke
Like history that's forgotten, black
Smoke, like the locked eyelids of the stones.

THE VAST IRIS

A huge eye enfolds me in its lashes,
Cuts off the outer light,
Draws me impetuously into is solar depths.
There, in its perfect circle,
History's raging animals surround me:
The shark, with its violent and shadowy finning;
The tiger, with eyes like bullets in flight;
Like the horror of a deadly purpose, the panther;
With a bloody avalanche of wind and talons, the eagle;
And the snake, with the poised ice of hate . . . ,
And behind, the long shadow of an endless dream,
The dark throng of looters:
The hyena, the vulture, the rats, the spiders,
The jackals and the glowing smoke
From a prairie of ants.
A circle without redemption, getting closer and closer.
Every species accuses me, keeps pouring out the inventory
Of my evils: I AM MAN!
I am all men.
I am the blind destruction.
The impossible hope.
The eternal enemy of all that exists.
I can hear thoroughout my blood the hum of stingers,
Claws, talons, jaws,
In the quivering iris
Where I am now prisoner — forever.

THE DREAM OF RETURNING TO CHILDHOOD

He walked into that wild valley
And childhood overtook him.
There was the same violent magic light,
The sheen of summer grass,
The clear mountains, the untamed birds,
The butterfly, the subtle rainbow of the falls.
That vision, so intimate, that dreamed him
Since he was a boy was his world, his matchless space.
Never could he discover that symmetry
Different from any other because all are
Different. Never that air just like others,
Nor that burgeoning beauty overflowing,
Nor that fragrance so deep in the folds
Of his beautiful memory. And though his return
Would have taken thousands of years, he would go on the same,
Not even men could ruin that recollection.
He saw the wind and the birds coming to greet him,
The leaves were filled with transparent tremors,
The wellsprings redoubled their restless song.
A fragrance of earth, fruits, waters and flowers
Floated through the air to meet him.
'He has come back!' hailed the voices of the valley.

THE WOMAN
FROM THE EARTH

Where? Where can she be?

Her body was the perfume
That gave a drunken air to the shadow and the night.
That shiver of water and silk
Whose rustling flamed up
From the keenness of touch.

Her eyes were light and tenderness.
The rousing voice
Splitting the half-light of the void. An answer
To desire. Two lives coals snatched
From the sparkling sea of summer.

With the shady wisdom of honey
And wines, her lips;
A lush petal. A garden.

Her neck was made of warm marble and rippling fire,
An arc in beauty's total silence.

But the tropical essence was her breasts.
Two pieces of fruit that kindled morning
With the fragrance of their open flesh
Spreading out to the sun.

With the whine and wind in the laurel,
The turning waist.
Vase of the flower.
The orange lull. Noon.

In the dizzy avalanche of kisses,
The bird of night,
A swarm of ecstasy.
Wave and winning foam. Bleeding
Quartz, crackling
Sunflower, untameable lightning,
A haven in which to hoard the universe.

THE YELLOW MOON

Like a fabulous coin of gold and mist,
Crater of a dark abyss
That would slowly, slowly, keep swallowing the world,
At the end of the quick slope,
Full of majesty, proud and all alone,
The great yellow moon.

Descending into the vortex of starry silence,
The birches flashing lightning,
The cyclopean firs,
The impetuous service trees,
Now pounce on us like blind panthers,
Like collapsing cathedrals of smoke,
Like towers of blazing shadow
That hardly graze us,
But the horse is a flame of water
Fatally beckoned by the moon,
Hypnotic decoy, swelling, trapping us
In the secret aura of the night.

THE DREAM OF SEX

Murky sex of shadow and desire
Feels and probes in the trembling brush
For the doorway to the abyss.
There the heart of frenzy pounds.
All the turbulence of dark splendor
Embracing, welcoming it to the deep.
It perceives the crash of waves,
The tossing winds that howl around it.
The void's invincible strength
Still threatening to assault,
Strip it of everything — destroy it.

You are all that groping phallus, imploring
With the humbleness of poverty alone.
With a hammer's perseverance, persisting,
Stubborn and feverish, ravenous and blind,
Thrusting, cleaving and, at last, lighting up
Silence with its fire. It enters, stays,
As though never, never, would the flame's
Heat end, its drunken thirst.
It knows: it's at the core of life.
Free happy master of each world
And all eternity.

THE EYES OF THE NIGHT

And the stars are overflowing,
Spilling their clear, drunken lights
Into the great gust of the night.
Those white disturbing stars,
Where the chasm in each man rises up,
Come slowly, descend like the faces
Of lovers that draw together.
With that same eternity,
With that same brevity and enigma,
The eyes of the night approach,
The teeth of jasmine, the sparkling fish,
The flowers of the light . . .
How they keep falling with blinding power.
How their thunderous music
Is the huge glow of space,
The dazzling wind that blows right to my window.

In this old house of glass and wood,
I notice its lure of a yearning siren,
The sweetest cosmic melody of light and water,
A shaking force that brings extermination.
Walled in by the huge birch tree,
This fragile and defenseless house
Wavers frightened
Before that mysterious green breast.
The stellar leafy branches
Loom near the window
And it is the dizzy gargoyle of the night,
A bottomless space emptying out.
A wild rippling of lava
Cleaving darkness sinks down deep.
Invasion of swamps,
Lichens, snowy magma underwater,
Lake depths of all that can be touched.
Hydras now surrounding the sleeper's bed.
Lying dreams!
Away with the night! Away with the shadows
Breaking the smooth surety of what is vast!
Harsh breathing, marrow of cold,
Roving psalmody of death.

The house begins to crumble,
Yet with a furious embrace
The tree lifts it up, and the wind, suddenly
Trembling, and the surprise
Of everything unnamed see the birch tree
Rise up from earth and carry in its branches
The dreams and lives of every man,
And with its long hair filled with stars
The birch tree soars through joyous airs
Like a sailing ship of fire suffused with songs.

THE CORPSE

The world's fragile shadows reach me
In these catacombs of hell.
Fragments of unattainable days soar high above.
Sweet distant voices like a thirst for clouds
Come back to me from gardens and memories,
Scorch me and make me remember the life I found
And all the life I might have had.

I feel the damnation and fire of my flesh.
This body slowly devouring itself
And turning rotten. In every heartbeat, in every sign,
In every death rattle, a shriek vibrates you cannot dislodge.

Now I am the pestilence from which men flee.

Damned and sunk into clays and rust,
Far from airy, transparent plants,
From the body bright and alive as a valley of heaven,
Listening to the waters' sleepless seeping,
The choking fumes of soft minerals,
Large drops of anguish, shadows' sluggish steam,
I remain in shrouding moisture and in silence.

MAYBE THE MIRE ITSELF

Like a rotten swamp
With neither insects nor germs, nor vestiges of plants,
Nor the passing of migratory birds above,
Nor even the far-off fleeing of the light;
With the bleakness of the absolute
Where fear or nostalgia does not exist,
Nor a place for the last desertion
For now not even grief has any meaning;
With a shadow that is not night or day,
And a silence that is already the drowsiness of nonexisting,
And a void bereft of empty space;
There where no change occurs,
Where nothing begets
Nothing, there in the midst of the mire,
With no other fixed boundaries
Than my darkness that cannot be diminished,
I stretch out in the sheer absence of life,
Anchored, buried, converted
Into dead eternity.

MADNESS

I feel shadows. Blue smoke of old grass
Runs through my veins, explodes in still feet.
My thoughts swell with remains of blood.
Their death rattles bellow between the fragile walls.
The house is walled off from light and voices.
Squalid maze where papers grow.
Doors fly open and birds squawk, trampled and unsightly.
Days, minutes, buried silence, slip by.
Eddies of dust eat away my mind,
Destroying colours, human architecture,
The world's logic, the world's memories,
Structures, windows, locked unhearing space.

There, far away, the cars are carrying corpses.
A world of corpses. But where are you?
Yes, yes, you are dead now. The house has forgotten you.
On the blind lamps I have hung your clothes by the neck.
They are only cobwebs thriving in the rooms.
From the lamps, you twist, livid, dead, hanged.
Bristling with fear, your body lives and dies.
Torment of shadows. Black surf. Vomit.
You are the corrosion of a painting that doesn't exist.

'Quiet! You're afraid!' the cobwebs say.
Smoke rises up through them. It comes from the mirrors.
They are the hidden doors of every enigma.
Papers whirl. The jungle of books springs up.
A blind multitude suffers, grows old and dies.
Groans in the glasses and in painted doves.
My hands are bats, they hunt me down with scissors.
My steps, a wild animal in jail. My fingernails scale
The walls, keep rising; teeth of vertigo gnash.
I pull up the floor tiles. Thick blood. Nobody.
Alone with myself. There, blindness under the earth.
There under the earth, alone with myself. Nobody.

THE TRAP OF TIME

I no longer feel my body against yours
Like a deep touch, entire. Subterranean
Years have kept on turning
Into dark and grotesque larva everything
That grew in the light. We have fallen
Into the trap of time, into that inherited
Defect, monotonous and pale.
The sewer of all our days
Keeps pouring weariness and renunciation
Onto our skin, onto the love that was.
A grey and dusty odour of rats
Bursts in on the ramshackle scene.
This poor memory is already mixing
Landscapes, humiliations, faces, deaths.
The future is now a sallow burst
Of laughter, a lean grimace,
A sheet of paper eaten by the years
Whose lines of love and their plans
Are now unreadable forever.

BETWEEN US RISE

Between us rise seas of black glass,
Chasms of quicklime, a typhoon of frozen sand,
White-hot walls, jungle denseness.

With an axe, they split open the eyes of tenderness.
Over them rolled trains of hate and resentment,
The sharpest needles in all surprises,
Sleepless indifference,
Rain of shadow and death.
Alone in the end, blind and stiff with fog,
Petrified with emptiness,
The eyes remained at the core of lifeless matter.

LIKE THAT PALE
WET SCRAP OF PAPER

Like that pale wet scrap of paper
That would scrupulously clean floors, bathtubs,
Polish metals, wake up the shadows
Of dead mirrors in a forgotten house,
Bitten by rain and the grossest dereliction;

Like that pale wet scrap of paper
That would clog drains and haemorrhages,
Torn by rust and scabs and cold,
Wearing out its essence in every touch,
Losing its size, turning
Into a rank, black and shapeless mass;

Like that pale wet scrap of paper,
Now crumpled, vile and stinking,
That no one's hands dare touch,
That no one's eyes want to see —
This is the dignity they've left me.

WHERE, WHERE DO WE GO?

When it dawns on us
That the memory of those days
Is almost nothing
And all that surrounds us
Cannot remain as it is;

When we know life
Robs us of everything;
A nagging sorrow shows us
How little lasting is love,
The bright pulsing of beauty,
The trusting ideas with which we raised a world;

When we see everything turns
Into sand darkly winnowed by time
And loneliness is filled with silence
That offers no solace or protection;

When we know before they arrive
That the lofty words
Cannot take refuge in the poem,
And they are only
Howls of anguish that race across our eyes;

When at last there is not even meaning
In this gesture of good-bye,
Where, where do we go?

ONLY THE UNCERTAINTY

Only the uncertainty of sensing
What may continue in another life
Prevents me from breaking up
This murky haze
Dividing me from death.
O frenzied doubt,
Turn into certainty,
Free me from the worst wickedness:
To go on being myself.

LONELINESS

Now he is alone
At the bottom of the alley of time,
In that long corridor
Of narrow walls, unsteady and elusive,
That are giant hands of smoke and leprosy.
There, sitting in the background
Like the shadow of a lifeless shadow —
The final wreckage of all that is human —
Without looking, he contemplates the world's collapse.
Amidst the wildest turbulence
A wind howls from under the earth,
Undermining everything,
And the corridor, like the broken bilge
Of a drifting boat,
Is battered by the vast night
Of all times. Thick gusts
Of blackness blow from the abyss,
And from the ground rises
The jagged chess play of fear.
Dark and alone,
Eyes unmoving,
Dry and distraught,
He listens to the death rattle that won't relent.

THE INSOMNIAC

He counts the green faces
Traced by the moisture on these walls,
The bread crumbs whose whiteness
Sows the table's grey sea with islands,
The steady, metallic advantage
Of the clock's heartbeat
Over the large raindrops of his bedroom,
The flashing spasms of the neon sign,
The stealthy cars sneaking over the dirty snow,
Some far-off voice,
The gurgling of hidden pipes
Like mutes caught by surprise,
The red and black letters
Stamped on the spines of books,
The gusts of wind, the sleet;
He counts the socks strewn on the floor —
Sleeping rats —
The empty bottles
Like chess bishops foreboding death,
The pale capsules,
Like a firing squad, lined up
Against never-ending night.

THE SUICIDE

Death's injection dissolves
With the last hope.
The birds and poplars return from far away.
All the faces converge, the gentle geography.
His body's dark rivers shudder.
He hears a slow and soundless voyage of needles,
A frozen bubble, a mirror and its shadow.
They advance and he cannot halt
The fever of their pace, their burgeoning growth,
Nor put to sleep the wounds they leave behind.
And he feels how the fire in his forest leaps up,
How the smoke climbs up around his eyes
And veins and blood burst with such a din;
How a strange sleeping wind wakes up
And a huge head sprouting from his chest.
His teeth are icy whirlwinds.
They are storms of vertical stones
Now aiming at the heart.

NOTICE TO THE TRAVELLER

Though you cannot stand the loneliness you shout,
Nor endure the emptiness of your hours;
Though your left eye is missing
And your right hand,
And you have no idea on which leg you walk;
Though you find yourself without hopes and strength,
And you see the light has lost its colour;
Though now the touch of flowers no longer matters,
Nor the water's laughter,
Nor the dazzling flight of birds;
Though children for you are
Stumps of shadow
And all the murmuring of humankind
A dark swell;
Though the history of men cracks
And breaks in your cold heart
Like a hide of filthiness and blood,
Remember that even
With the right eye or the left hand
Or what remains of your limbs,
You shall go forward
And struggle with all your blindness
Though for nothing else than to survive
For you are only a man.

MIRRORS HAVE ICE AND CHASMS

Mirrors have ice and chasms,
Windows of sleeplessness and searching;
Their steely vertigo sinks into us,
Leaving us in an alien reality.
The dream of their waters, of their feverish
Quicksilver, surges, approaches from afar
In a silent shout within the darkness
Which pain locks in and relentlessly erases.
It is life's coldness, the mirror's chill,
A deaf door, a stony nose, a slam.
In you, deep inside you, my life was drowning.
That faithful look of infinity
Which at times you furtively showed me,
That wind of jubilation and derangement,
Of frenzied desire and of love —
Where was its longing? Where the instants,
The laughter, the tender sensations,
The wide whirlwind of the bodies
With their sea and breath outspread?
Now all is chaos, for I behold
The travelled distance with forgetting eyes.
Eyes that sicken, pierce and blind
What they are seeing. Eyes that screech. Eyes
With a hanged man's gaze, with the delirium
Of orgies and everlasting rage.
Eyes that never take in what they observe, eyes
Also with the purity of everything untouched
That cannot even know why they shed their tears.
This world is dread itself, it is the uncertain
With nothing and no one to destroy it,
Nor can its primal order be restored.
Yet I am unable to escape, and here I stay
Bound to choking mirrors,
Sunk deep in their cloudy uncoloured glass,
In their wilderness of shadow and hollow places,
So near myself and so lost,
For I am not unaware that fear is my prison
And the mirror, the chasm of my hell.

THE WEEPING

Because there is nothing more than weeping,
Only weeping in the world,
The vertigo of grief, loss, decay,
And weeping, condemned crowds of people,
Emptiness and weeping, faces of fearless bitterness,
Forsaken and lost without knowing why,
And a trembling that grows like the depth of a chasm,
Weeping, weeping that fills the earth, trains,
Wine caves, weeping, jails,
Graveyards and weeping, ruins, weeping.
Just like a blind and never-ending invasion,
Like an overwhelming plague, the weeping,
Always the weeping, on the lonely beach,
In the cloudy silence of the afternoon,
Behind wet windowpanes and flaking walls,
In black cars, always the weeping, the weeping,
Monotonous, awful, unconsolable, captive,
The weeping, prayers, hospitals,
Orders, weeping, boots and rifles,
Weeping, misery, weeping,
Weeping along the sidewalks,
In the locked houses
Weeping, between fingernails and fingers and strands of hair,
Wetting chests, seeping into earth,
Drowning man, only the weeping, the weeping.

THE TUNNEL

Slowly he dragged himself through the narrow tunnel.
With fingernails, bile and blood, his hands stuck
To decaying stones of centuries and moisture.
He could not remember how he'd entered,
Who'd brought him, for what reason or punishment.
Hopelessly alone in time, in the dark
Echo, he slipped along like a strange slime
Spit by the shadows.
He went down into a relentless depth,
Into the steaming ooze of hidden places.

He began to make out an unseen breath,
A phosphorescent mass
That loomed up from far below.
In the fresh neighing of the fog
He racked his instinct to find traces
Of life, a sign, a conscious heartbeat
Which could break that silence,
That unequalled loneliness.

Impatiently he went on with the frenzy
Of finding a tiny life his senses
Could assume and share.
And full of faith and jubilation, with animal keenness,
With specks of blood in his gaze,
Tripping, searching with the instinct and sense of smell,
He went on falling into the black gulf. His ears began
To know a magma of tiny eyes
That glittered crackling with fury.
Like a sudden, accurate blaze, the deep,
Sticky plague reached him.

They were seas of hungry, burning spiders
That could not wait for his arrival.
They devoured each other with a bonfire's roar,
With a seething noise of dead leaves
And the hate of the abyss.
It was corrosive, defiling lust.
A dark, growing clamour awaited him.
A sluggish wave of shining pincers,
Of feelers and stingers, reached him:
His body was still.

He watched that white-hot ice draw near,
Black lava of claws, mouths, eyes.
He felt the crushing force,
And like an explosion of light and veins,
The blind sobbing of his wounded blood.

His body is cut to pieces
By that endless spasm of pain.
And that tunnel depth gives way and rains down,
And a storm of spiders keeps falling
And falling, overwhelming and constant,
In that corridor covered with spiders
That shall go with him, that always go with him,
That are now his eyes, his stomach and his voice.

NO NOISE, NO SILENCE

And suddenly, in my locked body dizzily
Cleaving the air, a dark chill.
A terrible impact explodes. The foam assails me
With sharp splinters, my silent, sleepless body
Plunging sleeplessly, plunging
Like a train without rails and headlights,
Reduced to bubbles in the sea of floating ice.
Now I am this thickness that shall never open,
Sinking in the unquenchable blackness,
Sinking and sinking.
Like rain or torrents they fall,
The dead keep falling from rivers and tombs,
From nights and crimes and forgotten centuries,
Revolving towers of eyes and rigid faces
Like columns, an icy museum
Of gestures, a cloudy vapour among veins of stone,
All eternity locked in the water,
Pale ripples almost glass,
Swinging slowness of lifeless hands,
Open mouths, masks that were made
Of old age and sorrow and this motionless smoke
That now fills everything.
Voids and shadows wound,
Disappear in darkness, dreams
Barely seen and cold whirlpools
From a circle of oblivion and dereliction,
Sudden scenes, the momentary sparkling of bones
On the backs of invisible steeds,
Smashing together and disintegrating, silent
Explosions, ships and skulls going down,
Sleepwalking cables and long
Hair cleaving masses of sunken ice, hiding
Huge forests, fossils, mirrors of bloodless matter,
The long descent of death
Going through passageways, narrow galleries,
Ocean currents, bilges and caverns, dropping
Into watery depths; eye sockets and clusters of hands,
Faded chains from which fingers emerge
Lit up by strokes of lightning,
But no noise, no sign,
No voice, no silence.
I am searching for the cry in my heart,
And I am searching in vain.

from
The Birch Tree in Flames
El abedul en llamas
(1978)

MOTHER EARTH

In the midst of a torrent
Of darkness and time,
In a sheer air
Of silence and oblivion,
You turn among the stars
Like the one garden
Of a lost universe.
In you, light and water,
Fires, greenery
And the land of aromas,
Are the holy body
Of your primal beauty.

You grant us life,
Offering yourself, transforming us
With the constant love
Of a continual forgetting.
So you call us
Perpetually, you breed us
From dust and waters,
As if we were only
This bold harmony
Dreaming of the landscape
And not the dark force
Of a destructive hate.

Little blue star,
Pollen from sea and forests
Of an intuited cosmos,
Mother of my universe,
From a bright corner
Of your earthly body,
Like one more witness
Of the fleeting stay,
You write my poem.

WATER

I hear it gush in fountains,
A white rush of freshness
Filling the air with beauty.
Its clear wings
Come down over earth and, opening,
Are the eyes of the world,
The joyful ringing of everything unchanged.
The sun floods it with languid sheens.
To learn its enigma
Birds quietly draw near,
And man gazes,
Wanting to feel all its innocence.
He invades its stillness.
He goes into it and looks at himself,
Hugs, drinks,
And now he lives the peace
Of his quieted thirst.
From its foaming body
He emerges into the full light,
Springs up clean once more,
Happy child and king of the created.

THE BOY AND THE STONE

At the core of the day
A boy watches the sun beam down from the clouds.

With a white stone he aims
Toward the cresting of the waves
And smiles at the light caressing him.

He hurls his hard stone against the summer sea
And from his hands springs up,
Like a gust of wind, noon.

With its salty tongue the stone leaps
Over the foam, opening up bright spaces.

The seagull twists its slow flight.
A ship's siren exhausts the horizon.

Then he sees the ember of the stone drown,
The bird vanish into the blue verge
And the boat become a dot and disappear.

Soon he shall know the slightest distance
That exists between happiness and sorrow.

THE SEA

Magnetic green body of darkness and abyss,
With the high horses of foam
It hurls its power of pursuing mystery
Through the night and days of Earth.
At times it sleeps, flowing slowly onto beaches
As if it would retrieve in its dereliction
An old dream of seaweed and coral,
Skies of drunken stars and far-off stories
Of ships and myths sunk in its depths.
Wildly it reaches our ears
With a crashing now we'll never forget.
Maybe it is a god or monster waking.
It never stops, for its soul
Is ceaseless unrest and motion.
And it bubbles and bellows, shining forever
In a burning beauty that cannot be destroyed.

THE DAYDREAMING AIR
OF LATE SUMMER

With their delicate flames
The butterflies cloud
The daydreaming air of late summer.

The towering light plays in the cypress's
Silver leaves, and sleepwalking bees
Buzz beside the airy heliotropes.

Dragonflies of sun
Dance in the twilight good-bye to the afternoon.

My life is still as young as summer's
And has no wish to think that the warm, frail moss
Welcoming me today will be a tooth of cold.

THE TRUTH OF BEAUTY

In the vast loneliness, at the foot of the hill,
I sought the shady coolness of the trees.
The painful brightness cracked the hide
Of that country, untamed and harsh,
Where I could most feel the language of the blood.
Suddenly I could not see the sun. Two jet-black wings
Of fire hid it from view. The silence scanned
Its majesty, and there high above, an eagle
Of sun stared at the world. Everything remained
Expectant: the ochre earth, the olive groves,
The huge blue torrent of the sky,
The cheerful bushes, the grim thicket,
The rocks and their diamond eyes;
And that sun was now the eagle and its feathers, light.
Time stopped.
How long did the image last? I shall never know.
And yet that memory has been
Forever the truth of beauty.

BIRCH TREE

Stem of fleeting light
Caught in a slow net of butterflies.
You are the green gust wounding sun.

Like tired smoke
You alight in the blue,
With the water's siesta
Shining in your leaves.

In your body's winged spiral
The wind travels and delights,
Trembles in your transparent form
And raises you on fire to my dreams.

ON A SACRED SUMMER'S DAY

The wild duck
Unfolds its coloured presence
And slides through the solemn truth
Of the lake. The waters open their blue
Rings and surround
The bird's gladness with a sound
Almost past hearing, as if they were afraid
To startle it in their smooth folds.
The mallard gleans the rainbow of the sunset,
Cares only for its lordly swim.
Far from the gaze of that man,
It cannot conceive that it, too, is
A meagre reference of light
On a sacred summer's day.

IN HAPPINESS

Near autumn's frontier
Summer's heat
Still demurs at departing.

Stretched out in the grass,
Through shady branches
I see how the stars
Of sun go deep.

The cicadas strum
The song of summer.

With their green sails
The fir trees sway
In time to the breeze
Like a clipper ship moored in the plain.

In the rye the wind
Paints gold horses
In a sparkling yellow sea.

The grass trembles, the sun,
The branches of shadow,
The breeze, the whole field;

And in the blazing density of afternoon,
From fire to joy
Our bodies bind, grow, climb.

ANOTHER BURNING DISTANCE

To raise a blank sheet of paper and see the poem,
As if my gaze could probe
Another burning distance where it was written
By the hand of a chance that precedes me.
To cross through the dense forest of sight
With a keen and dogged gleam.
And so, with the calm of controlled fire,
To keep it in its future truth,
I start to retrieve the mysterious lines
Of that other presence slipping away
In the blinding light of its origin.

ONLY A DROP OF DEW

A drop of dew falls
On the whisper of a petal.
For an instant it stays hanging
From an edge of water and light.
It leaps into the void and is a kindled planet
In the passion of pearl and sapphire.
Newborn ember that slips
Over the flower's idle tongue,
Like the beautiful, disturbing image
Of our blue star in the universe.

FOREIGNER

Some far-off noise
Like an alms reaches my ears.
Three in the morning
Or is it the declining afternoon that moans
Blackness? This silence . . .
Only silence and snow.
Time creaks in the furniture of the house
And a dry mist lingers in my eyes.
From the end, from the beginning,
The days slip by, and my whole life,
In this hostile, inexplicable winter.
One day I shall go back,
Once and for all.
I shall go back to the south, the south,
To the radiant myths of childhood.
I shall go back to being a god lit up by the sea
And the blue shade of the grove.
And I shall laugh in the songs of fragrant air,
Impulsively, among wine and guitars,
With old friends,
Living among my people,
Feeling in gushes
The blood's uproar and delight,
As though I could never again be
A foreigner, lost, lonely and sad.

GRAND CANARY

There you are, awaiting me in the South,
Like a hard topaz hewn by the sun.
In the Norwegian cold I spy your gaze
Of perennial palm and the gold glitter
Of your beaches. Altitude aloft, light, pyramid
Of lava and glass, from the Atlantic
You rise up like life toward love.
Your white springtime of almond trees and longing
Crosses this fog surrounding me
And then you arrive, fervently,
With your salty, volcanic breeze,
With all your landscapes and music,
And so, island and passion of my wandering road,
You console, keeping me from grief and forgetting.

ARTUR LUNDKVIST

Like an oak ablaze or a volcanic dream,
He spurts from the planet's wound
In a spilling of light, sperm and bronze.
He is bound only by life for he was born to burn.
He is made of passion and air. An embattled truth.
Rooted to earth, doggedly dreaming it,
He sinks his roots into song,
Making us one with his lashing.
His eyes are of broken water, his thirst the wind's.
He asks freedom for its permanent height.
He grows like grass protecting prairies,
Carving in the blindness of silence
The warning of death facing the future.
His books are forests in motion,
Fragrances of forgotten cultures,
Tenderness of the rivers on humble flowers,
The irrevocable music of his love for Earth.
There in the North he follows his feeling for roads
In the seventieth year of his life of fire.

THE POET

To know yourself uprooted
Without thinking why,
Far from the useless game
Of fame and hierarchies,
Feeling you rob
Or disturb no one's air;
To be alone, devoted
To the diaphanous craft
Of a minute art,
With the gentle patience
Of starting each day
Braiding words
Into columns of light.
To reconcile the past
And the uncertain future
With the image of the dream
We had then,
Loving each term,
Seeing in their signs
Our deepest voice,
And to accept the choice
    Of this unlucky fate:
The failure and the flame.

THE TAMER
Homage to Octavio Paz

The tamer took his place in the ring,
In the midst of the silence and people,
Before the chasm of life
And the judgment of men.
He came from the sun and brought a mirror
Of wild transparencies
And a secret legacy of intelligence and light.
His face lined with grave strength
Projected the proud eyes of a stern
Forsaken breed,
To which he, perhaps better than anyone,
Gave clarity and vigour, feeling and a way.
Many, and every day more,
Came from different latitudes and races
With the sole aim of learning his command.

Suddenly the tamer revealed some frenzied birds
That opened up a bright and hidden vertigo,
And from his hands sprang wild beasts with sluggish movements
Exploding with a flash of beauty in the mind.
Butterflies of sun as gentle as smiles
Or fish probing with blades of fright.
Strange animals crossing from mystery
To silence, discovering its imprisoned blood.
And those others that stirred up dreams
And visions that few could hope to glimpse.
All the animals of language
Sporting their splendour,
Becoming horizons, flames, flight and existence,
Loveliness unleashed, and power,
Before the blue gaze of their master.

RAQUEL

In the pure silence of the room
We're left alone.
From your few months,
You look at me, unknowing, almost joyful,
With your bright, steady gaze,
As though you still had the secret
Of a place beyond all space.
Your tiny hands,
Like two wings of freshness and light,
Grasp my fingers.
In your face beams
The first innocence man's
Life must have had
When only confidence existed,
A blind tenderness, and love was whole.
But you cannot speak to me.
I only listen to your voice
Pursuing words.
It echoes tinkling
Between white walls.
You are here with me and, in your eyes, you link
The goodness of the pure and the petite.
At that moment you laugh and share with me,
And in your fragility I feel protected
And I don't listen to the street,
Nor to troublesome day beginning.

CANDALABRAS OF WINTER

There they were, at each end of the table, singing
Melodies of love against the winter.

They had five arms, five silver dreams
That firmly held the blazing
Unfurled tresses of the gods.

To stay next to them
Was to be in the shadow of magic.

And the conversation grew more vibrant,
The silence more subtle.

In the faces they created a lasting hue,
As though, from baroque centuries, they were painting
Grace, surprise and harmony.

From memory's dark patina springs
Their beauty's sheerest joy,
Ensnaring the splendour of fire.

NORDIC WOMEN

Bodies of goddesses, dense gold bodies,
Bodies where pearl and light are kindled
With glimmers of swan and moon and quiet sea.
Bodies in which the youth of heaven soars,
The arrogance of blinding snow.
Bodies of burning marble,
Of indelible freshness, radiant
As branches of water and sun on sand.
Bodies with crystalline breath,
Transparence of leaves,
Crossing my nights, dazzling my days.

Firm bodies of Nordic women
I knew in places that gave me
The forest splendour,
The waves of rye, classrooms, trains,
Basalts of mist and hollows,
Or in summer's naked afternoons
Beneath the service tree's light shade.
Bodies of smoothness born from the breeze,
With the swift contentment of waterfalls and rivers
Passing over my skin, loving in my memory.

AURORA BOREALIS
IN ICELAND

I walked out on the balcony after the power of love
And gazed again at the room in darkness.
Sigrun's glowing body
On vanquished sheets,
Her languid red hair
Slipping down asleep to the rug.
In early morning fullness, I inhaled
That gentle weariness reconciling me to life.
My breath left fleeting faces of smoke
Pierced and destroyed by a maddened wind.

With a backdrop of ice and volcanos
Reykjavik hoarded its autumn stirrings.
Now it was the frontier of night or morning.
That misty darkness
Had its own trembling, a sudden start,
Not wind growing wilder, nor hard frozen sea.
It was the birth of another light,
Light starting to spring from itself.

Huge white strips emerged from a delta
Awesome and majestic.
Its breadth travelled the firmament.
Floods of shining spirit
Overran the branches of the air.

Bursting colours bound me to their giddy altitudes,
Silent outcries of green daybreak.
Blues and yellows unfolded,
Replete with abundance, a golden mauve rose high,
Impossible violet, glad orange,
Ochres of fire and amber, swift, legendary,
And the colour of sky, of snow, of light with further light.

Suddenly the unchecked colouring
Seemed to halt its cosmic joy.
The cold made it grow still, trapped it
In its invincible prison, giving body to its light.
Eyes, icy and intense, loomed up in the mist,
Music staffs, sails, flags,
Embers and blossoms of locked light
Cruising on the heights,
Kindling the never-ending domes.

Years have passed, so swift and slow.
Maybe most of what I have lived
Is just experience repeated,
Growing lost in my being and its memory.
And yet I shall never forget
Sigrun's sleepy smile waking
To the aurora borealis of Iceland.

from
Otesnita
(1979)

OTESNITA

When I then began seriously
Not to ask hope for any life,
She arrived with a fervour almost of adolescence.
Her eyes pierced my astonishment
Like a hard flash of lightning
Suddenly set free
In my loneliest and most defenseless dreams.
I never beheld a face
So wrought with tenderness and silence.
And the ripe fragrance of fruit
And the unfathomable breath
Left by clear water in the breeze
Joined in springing from her lips.
Her body was made of flight and innocence,
Wings offering me
The burning jubilance of flowers.
Nights passed, waves, seasons, and one day,
From the glitter of chance,
A new word appeared among words:
Otesnita . . . and I said it again: Otesnita.
Gradually it was invaded by a dazzling love
And it took refuge in her eyes,
Opened heavens in her laugh
As we laughed, laughed
As only children
Dare to or those that love this life,
For at that instant I knew
That would always be her name.

GAZELLE OF WATER

You arrived limpid as a gazelle of water
That would suddenly spring up
In the night forest of my body
And turn my bleak prison
Into a blazing lamp.

I have lived
The gadflies of hate and disgrace,
Blameworthy negligence,
My defenseless promises and their dreams.
I have seen cathedrals of shadow rise up,
Of vanity or lies, and preserved
The insatiable hope of waiting for you.

Let us live this never-repeated urge,
Knowing that after our fire
Only fear and ashes will remain,
The desolation, the rain and the forgetting.

Hug me, for only your embrace
Gives me the image of the earth, the water,
Conquered space, the word and the music,
The warm radiance of grasses,
You, unique, blue planet, world all my own.

ONENESS IN THE FIRE

It glows like a torch
That, instead of crackling, would pierce
With seething tenderness
The moist open rose of the night.
It is a sea of stallions
And lips without measure,
A galloping of blood, earth, and fire,
A tumultuous river
That toward the chasm of your womb advances,
Retreats and goes on amidst fever, denseness,
Branches, light, shadows, clay,
And at last it is transformed
Into the aroma of sun that is life.

TO SEE YOU

To see you, to see myself in your eyes and feel
Your unleashed laughter
Like the sacred home of Earth.
I receive from your hands and from your lips
This fire offering magic and order, a road
For my boundless heart.

I listen to your words
Like a shower of light,
Tiny from their simplicity.
With what fresh tenderness
You give me open-handedly
Translucent loyalty,
Jubilant kindness and truth.
Because you are the longing in every distance,
Your presence with greater yearning rises in my blood
And the splendour of the world amidst your body.

IN ALL THE PLACES

Among harassing mists,
The vertical beauty of the pines.
Autumn's blurred vastness quivers,
Broken by the watery voices
Of children racing over joyous grass.
The fullness of their frolic
Reaches even the brooding distance.

Unsure, I ask myself what you would be
Before we knew each other,
And memory ransacks my childhood
For shining days to lend them your face.
It is your body, too,
In the early bodies of desire,
Drawing me towards your young flame
To be all the time that has lasted in me.

Silence slowly turns into stone.
Coldness of stone hurled by the night.
Like nuts of the piñon pine, the children grow dark.
The wind awkwardly blows deep among the trees
While the water falls silent in mirrors of shadow.
Mists, winds rising up to the exact height
Of yourself, and my eyes feel nothing anymore
But the glowing air left by your memory
Wherever my injury lives.

LONELINESS
AMONG THE SANDS

The seagull glides down and halts
In the crystal of the air
Like a tear searching for a face.

The night breeze
Draws near with stars. The sea unfolds
A wordless sobbing that death has taught it.

Trees bowed and
Bitten by the thirstiest light and salt.

Loneliness among the sands. The cold
Of the first shadows grows.

Only her absence
Burns in the dark earth.

DYING WORLD

I walk in the sands
Beneath the light of dead stars.

Within its still shadow
Life becomes depraved.

Insistence howls
At an indifferent sea.

She is devised by my look
And preserved by the air.

Nothing silences the pain
Of a fiery void.

Untouchable presences
In the burnt gold.

A body without mercy
That memory strips bare.

A footprint snatched by the wind
And left in lies.

THE UNMOVING DISTANCE

More and more defenseless, the days
Die out in themselves,
For neither questions nor desires invoke
That shadow. I feel her
Remain immobile,
Her back to her light.
A cold breeze stirs the curtain.
My gaze grows lost
In the grey expanse.
It looks and waits for nothing.
It only wears out in the distance
Of the living that was loved, of the dead far away.

NEVER WITH POSSESSION

Never love with the locked impetus
Of any possession,
For what springs up from you would be a sterile growth.
You would only suffer
From silent death stalking it.
If all is change and nothing remains in what it is,
Do not deliver this unstable yearning
To what can only be the flower of an instant.
You have before your eyes the whole sea outstretched,
The earth lit up and its adventure.
Everything shines, reflects within you, calling.
Live its frenzy
While the slender air of afternoon
Benignly reaches your raised forehead,
For you know by love and beauty
Your new certainty cannot be disturbed.

THE SEA'S VISIT

On the rocks' green rust
I know I wait for a miracle.
Images in the water come and go.
Its waves lift glassy temples.
Diamond regions
Smash hard against black basalt,
Leaving the breeze
Spangled with snowy almond trees — quivering.
Their enamels barely turn
In the wondrous mirror of the sun
And to the waters they return like lost rain.
Now the unceasing suicidal horses go back.
They are a perfect unity. Closeness.
A crystal vapour leads them.
It reaches me, winged with majesty.
It unfolds in colours
And says: 'I was waiting for you as well.
Let us talk for a long time,
But first, live and dream your day among men . . . '

THE ROOSTER

The rooster springs from sleep and is dawn
Advancing in the village square of colours.
Now his song redeems life still asleep
In the hostile silence of the inert.
And he quivers and cries out,
Lifting a hard jet of energy
Whose fist smashes
The shadows' lurking breath.
Against that thick wall of death
He hoists his bonfire.
It is the faithful glare's wave and foam
Freeing the state of waking.
Fury and screech of glass,
Of metals and spilling lights.
Clarion of pride and power
Where thirst affirms:
The truth of being alive. And so, wild
And erect at the crack of daybreak,
Alone facing day while all is sleeping,
A fountain of shuddering height exalts,
Calling morning to touch and fragrance,
And like a ship in space
Whose sails bear all the ocean and its dreams,
It floods my eyes with the sun's song.

THE POET'S WINNING DAY

The look's devoted craving
Before day turning unfurled in itself.
Throbbing foundation of colour.
A hummingbird in flames slowly reveals the world.
His unbridled faith lights origins
In the thirsty streambeds of summer.
Impossible to halt his winning sequence.
The light rises towards the sun among glass trees.
Fleeting transparencies reach the eyes
In intermittent scenes of bluest greenery.
An oracle mounts from mists of earth.
The lone ear of wheat
Places a gold drop in the midst of my forehead,
Like a planet showing in its wonders
Stillness awake and motion.
The river dreams sacred syllables
Far and near, inside my blood.
I am just an instant in space,
A shadow living in the flower of the fire,
The battlefield of a free thought,
Lucidity of zeal:
A word that vouches for the life of man.

THE VISITOR

Before I heard footsteps on the stairs,
An acrid odour of iodine, fish and seaweed
Suddenly rose among my papers.
But I paid no heed.
I went on breathing
The ephemeral flight of signs
In their high meadows.
Insistently the doorbell
Raised questions in every corner.
At last, unavoidably, I opened.
It was an old man, naked and wrinkled
By the salts of time or the abyss.
On his head he wore
A crown of dawning water,
And in one of his scrawny hands,
A trident cut from coral light.
His gaze was proud, his voice most humble:
'I have come to give you the last thing I own.'
From his nets he drew a tiny sea
And spread it out to the hallway's astonishment.
The house was flooded beneath the indigo
Nerve of his lightning bolts.
Furniture, books, objects, thoughts,
Began an unpredictable dance.
Not even their shadows could escape.
They went off, emerged from far away,
Climbed so close
That downwards they shyly fled
Amid the slender skipping of boyish foam.
'Forgive me,' said I. 'My health
Won't allow this briny moisture.'
Then, bewildered, he called in his sea,
Set it on his back once more
And went off tearfully towards life.

THE MAGICIAN'S WING

As I wake these watery lines,
A blackbird, a fear, sings.
It sings from now to now.
Its words are stones
That in a void sleep,
Wake and burst.
You hear them fall
Like impatient and forgotten thunderclaps
Down to a smooth silence
Of hermetic mountains.
From the mountains springs
A pale hand.
The hand, growing larger, flies, displays
A garden in its palm,
And within the garden
The sheer darkness growing light.
O flower of intense snow,
Daily, sculpted rose
In bodies of prodigal grove,
Where the signs are born, multiply
Like gunshots or whispers,
On account of a hand
With which a fear writes
And in which a blackbird sings.

IN THE WATERS OF THE SUN

In a leap of fury,
The horse rose from unexpected air,
Toppling his linked shadow.
Sudden, carved in white-hot marble,
He scorched clear space.
And he glistened in the wind, sparkled among the trees.
All things living treasured his beauty's new
Sword plunging into the waters of the sun.
The mirrors of the lake woke
At that fiery joy springing
From a kingdom of foam.
A neighing higher than afternoon
Spread its pride in the distances.
And naked and happy as the light,
He crossed the grass and freely tried the world.

A RAIN OF BLUE SYLLABLES

The rain of blue syllables falls.
Leaves and grasses wake.
All their glory remains erect,
Lived in flower, in tree, in mute aromas
Flowing through riverbeds of afternoon.

Now the blue rain burnishes black stones,
Gently opening them from their hard cores.
It touches their imprisoned flesh, freeing and baring it
In corollas of reddened pulp.

Sap invoking sun, sun scything the rain.
Ruthless fire parching the slender green,
Meadow choking in barren furrows,
Red petal dying in rock,
Rock closing, captive to itself,
Falling silent, deaf and black till the miracle:
Till brazen spring arrives,
Bringing us a rain of blue syllables.

TOWARDS ANOTHER FREEDOM
Homage to Icarus

Nor were words enough.
Yet behind the world he heard
The airs of the street, syllabics of voices,
Slow, numerous footsteps headed
Toward their daily destruction.
He viewed himself among oppressed beings,
Sinking in the factories of Monday:
They traded freedom for grey survival.
Hidden in hollows of silence,
He fled so they wouldn't find him
And remained alone in the city
Ecstatic with sun.
The parks rose
With blue flocks of pigeons.
The trees newly loved by the rain
Revolved with their green jewels.
Clean sounds, nimble, happy . . .
He lived in the images
But was not calmed by that constant festival.
He made his way toward new distances
Where sea and red space merged.
Gradually he was reaching the highest peak.
He slowly watched the horizon
Till he felt rapture in his blood.
It was uplifted by the abyss.
He started up toward the light,
Winning the warm air.
An unforeseen force beckoned
Through regions of roving lightness.
He crossed the wonders of flowing colours
Revealing their naked clarities,
And he climbed, climbed toward the garden of the sun
Till he became the one freedom.

AND THERE, THE SEA

And there, in a moment's cleanest astonishment,
It seemed to be waiting since the hidden origin,
Or in another human life I might have lost.
In its restless expanse, it shone
With delirious verdure, with every murmur,
And in the dark, clear cavities of the water.
It revealed the presence of the unknown
When reaching the beach blazing
With the flowers of a jubilance in breakers
And hurled down clouds set at our feet.

From the swaying forest rises
A blue motion of greedy branchworks
Springing from the rumbling gulf of its enigma.
Suddenly it's a silence of prairies
To hurl singing sails of vertigo
Against the unruffled doggedness
Of the rocks. It brings me the uproar
Of its unmoving memory. Old man and child, it gazes
From its timeless age. Nothing in it remains.
Exiled from its sprawling distance,
Unfeeling and alone, it goes out and returns,
Bursting toward the limit from unvanquished wonder.

THE HAWK'S FLIGHT

The eye of the hawk emerges from space
And makes the mountain that conceals it disappear.
A radiance, unconquerable, keeps extending its image.
Trees like dreams stretch out their useless arms
In the presence of his storm.
Lightning bolts of sun disappear
Dark, defeated
By the hot stream of his flight.
The forest is transformed into a puddle of leaves
Forgotten in the air.
Everything watches and wonders at the furious ascent.
Neither the spears nor nets of rain reach him.
Nor the dogged hunter's finger of death.
Only the hawk crossing the sky,
Circling toward its unrelenting magnet.
Its lofty transience is what lasts.
From always to now,
An avalanche of summoned wind hurls down
And into memory sinks its talons and dizzy heights.

THE TIGER STEALS FORTH

Through thickness he steals forth without a sound
And the jungle falls silent.
In his fur gold blazes,
The night's green flashes
And a trapped gale throbs.
Sudden velvet shadow, electric
In its swift design,
Goes fatefully in search of its prey.
From his eyes' yellow forge
An intolerable beam paralyzes,
But in them also lingers
And lives the red river becoming dusk
And a blue violet lithe among grasses.
The antelope's watery jet
Breaks the silence.
A solar ship and claws bring it down.

From any distance the roaring of a ruler can be heard.

FACING THE ABYSS
OF THE BLANK PAGE
Homage to Stéphene Mallarmé

Between the bare page and myself
The seagull of dizziness descends.

Only the rustling of this future
And the silence gleaming
With the promise of plenitude.

And all the questions keep falling
Into its lost depth.

Now life is reconciled with the infinite.

In that clean gaze the eye drowns
Beneath the white shadow
Of a sea hurling names at the hostile transparence.

THE RED ROSE

Slow chain of days,
Anonymous weeks and months unfolding
In the weary city's locked limits.
And in the middle of the night the wind's throbbing,
With a whisper of depths, surf and sand,
Brought me a fragrance, invincible nostalgia.
I lifted my eyes toward the moon
And saw the sea of my island call me,
Seeking me in my dream, ordering me to return.

I gradually went back to the land of my birth
From the blue space of that flight.
I watched the sky blazing in the beauty
Of the island's golden peaks.
The sea recaptured its pure transparence,
The burning reverie of other times,
And it raised that world in its round borders.
I felt its hand rise and lower me
Toward the desert of a dazzled south
As though the whole island offered me its anxiety.

In the recovered distance,
There on the height of Mount Lentiscal,
In its oasis of secluded shade,
My parents' old house is dreaming.
I left the gate ajar and then relived
The kingdom of verdure. A crystalline freshness
Breathed in every corner,
Reaching me like a prophecy,
As though earth and tenderness recovered
The peaceful love waiting for me there always.

I almost touched the air. I lived in the aromas.
The lofty pines of my childhood
Surrounded me in their motionless dance,
Rising amidst the ivy towards space.
Heady essence of moon and water
From ilang-ilang, jasmine and magnolia.
And butterflies, fruits and a frenzy of birds.

I walked. But suddenly, there near the porch,
Below a background of whitewash and vines,
Over the parched lawn,
All became silence:
                    only the rose.

From what volcano, from what holy lava
Did you sculpt your lightning in its fire?
The breeze made you used to its dress,
So you are a loving swell,
Red impulse, aura of sun. Venus
Emerging from the petals of an endless sea.

I lift you between my fingers to look at you.
I go up to your lips and you are the brightness
That was waiting. A symbol of life.
Clean star-studded sun covering me completely
In this unexpected welcome.

All that I was not or am,
Even my future landscapes,
Utterly everything standing to extol you.
O ruby sparkling untameable joy,
Touch of velvet or lethargy of pearl,
Sensual nave, corolla of convulsive lights,
You spring from the mild moment between pleasure and sleep
Like the simple light that is shared.

Only the pulse of your fragrance explains you.

You bud and flare up
On the eve they decide your sentence.
Your fullness like our lives
Is extinction born on the day when we begin.
Ceaseless in the air and in the earth,
You reappear with the name of your kind,
And you are eternal now in this mute instant
Because more time is not greater eternity
And memory proceeds from death.
Night opens its coffer of tiny sounds:
A late bumblebee, the breeze in the branches,
The sleepless dribble of a fountain,
Shadows adrift disappearing in the dark . . .
Quietly I go back towards the house.

And it's hard to say I'm on the verge
Of tears for the life of a rose.

AGE

To feel ourselves scorned and to suffer
The vast spill of spring
In the scorched jungle of lonely age.
To see your fiesta fall once more
Into the mute spaces
Of a land condemned to night,
While distant days,
With a butterfly's fatal tracery,
Seek in vain a breeze in flames.
Yet let's accept
The harsh tattoo
Used by smokey years to brand our skin,
And celebrate our grope for life,
That gorgeous rapture of fleeting time.

IN THE NAME
OF OUR OWN VOICE

Blindly we started getting used to
Expecting help from the dead.
Yet the dead don't love us.
In shadows, they slip away.
The bodies of roots that once lived us
Fade away in devoured silence.
And since strong men and their norms
Filled us with apathy till scorn,
We went on turning into a chill of statues.
Locked in noises,
Between bitter walls of sadness,
Finally
We knew ourselves forgotten and alone.
Alone before a choking tear,
Alone before the void of a vertigo drying
The little blood still
Questioning
            furiously
                        with our own voice.

NIGHT IN THE CRY

With its icy lance
It crosses windows,
And in its deerlike flight
Strikes stillnesses,
Kindling forgotten memories
Of crazed insomniacs,
Scaring suicides,
And in a fathomless dream
Making children more alone.
It goes on toward an inaccessible fate
Amidst naked islands of shadow.
With lacerating light
The cry invades us,
Opens eyes and threats
And suddenly extends
That hounding touch.
It quivers, explodes and flies
With a swirling slowness
Occupying and growing
Beyond the limits
Of the last frontiers,
And from there it keeps on
Travelling and burning
The farthest valleys
Of unreachable
Dreams, and from there
It approaches and pursues
Other dreams covering
The greatest distance
And even greater, much greater,
Till a distance
So near that all of us
Would hear the cry
Crossing, raised by
The silence of fear.

THE ONE GEOGRAPHY

I look for the body I will never keep again
In the most vital core of lightning.
That one born in the embrace itself
When the skin flares
With that transparence we forget.

I look for all the love I look for no longer
Though, despite me, I go on believing
In the unvarying light of its chimera.

I look for the most simple, its clear secret:
The blaze of your smile among the willows,
Your seasons' hidden caresses,
The sunny harmony of our steps together
In the confiding truth of days.

And though I may never find it, I will look
For a home held in miracle,
With that unquenchable permanence
Of mountains and rivers and roots
Whose distance writes the horizon.

I look in the brief lines of my hand
For the answer — seeing you till death
And decoding a time
Where we shall have to be
The one geography of a changeless sea.

THE POISONER

You will never know the risk you run
When reading these lines,
For though you go over them idly,
You will start to hear with haste or sorrow
How its row of ants increases in your eyes.
This unavoidable calligraphy
Merging with the thick juices of your past,
Or winging in the burning plumage of your dreams,
Is now part of you like your blood,
With its flow of time in your memory.
And yet you have no idea that these dark drops
Leave you the poison of the poem.

PAPER BARS

With stubborn pain
I lifted this lament seered
By words in the futility of my hours.
In this insanity pages grew
Like a prison shackling white-hot hands of want.
I no longer knew how to live, or even escape.
Everything gradually shrank to a scant script
Of observed light, to this oppressed thirst
Behind blind bars of paper.
I learned to breathe in the dark space
Of the world's echoes left within me.
And only the devoured memory
Between the reality of appearance
And the moveable truth of dreams
Lent its meagre pulp and gaunt freedom
To what could have been fullness and flame.

THE FREEDOM OF
THE PERPETUAL PRISONER

He recognizes a dogged hate
Dissolved his caution,
For he dares to dream against the silence.
He listens beyond the bars to the bustle in the square,
The people migrating in their greedy trade.

He dreams out of depraved fatigue,
Imagining a vague horizon that isn't there.
He foresees the tracing of its seething chimera:
The dauntless sails steering
Toward the lofty fragrances of a world redeemed.

And he leans over, humiliated, for he understands
He is wrong in his raving
And freedom is always the word;
The lie affronts.

He knows man lives to go on being mistaken
And to abandon all the answers
His courage could offer.
With the years, his prison will grow smaller.
He will be only a mouth chewing its own oblivion.

THE CONDEMNED MEN

Each one despairs of covering
Cavities of wind opened up in their insides by age
Till they dry.

They grow silent starting with their shadows.
Only a seething of grief turning into a cloud of smoke,
And yet they advance against chance and fear.

They cannot rest on or take refuge in
The false game of their promises.

Spying an opportunity, they watch each other, distrusting.
At times they feel peace within their bodies
Wander in love or discover death.

They go on crowded, seeking one another, falling or dreaming,
Though they will never reach, however much they try,
The warm city that would give them shelter.

While being scorned by scant time,
They flow without respite into locked stillness,
And soon they're turned
Into the brief lie of having been.

THE BLACK TREE

Winter's faded colours
Blur in the watery depths
Of his gaze. He feels the cold scent,
His memory's white nakedness
Like a ghost that would never stop
Crossing through his mind.
In the tower howl unknown voices,
A savage shower piercing the mist,
And that other silence:
The void behind everything
Offended by death.
And a black tree, essence of maimed and burnt members,
Slides the agony over his body.
Its presence injures the valley's grim waste,
And only a bellfry without bells
Remains expectant from its own ruin.
Behind its hollows of shadow,
Its windows corroded with rust,
Closed eyes stare at the vile desolation.
No one, he sees no one, senses no one.
Life is this locked grave
In which only rotten memories lie buried.
Prisoner of this landscape tied to himself,
Growing deep in himself,
Each day he hears the tower's winds,
The long absence of words,
The mist's uneasiness he fails to understand,
And he looks at that blind tree, constantly blacker,
Which very soon must be his one fixed vision.

STONE

Death and its language always stalk
From the stone's hardest depth.

The grass is struck dumb, uprooted
By its sudden threat. With a sphinx's aridness,
Stone leads us to superstition
And a flood of hatred. Far or near it waits
For the blood's most vital warmth.

See it anchored in the night,
Filling the place where day sings.
It longs to be the surprise blinding us
In that impregnable
Silence of being stone among stones.

AVATAR TOWARDS IMMOBILITY

When he discovered her in the silence,
She dazzled him from her nakedness.
Her eyes took on the features of refuge
Where mildness was created.
Her body, a constellation of surf,
Started to climb in its tremor of fire
And seek him and depart from that doorless thirst:
The harmonious calm of the canvas where she was.

He divined her; heard her craving call
Amidst a garden of imprisoned lights;
And that smooth hand, barely suggested,
Seemed to rise, whisper, invoke him
From another reality where vision
Was already the first step towards the unforeseen.
He understood the subtlety of her proposal:
To exchange this way the wandering of his dull days
For the stillness of the happiest moment.

He felt her invade him
With that strange determined power
Only total love
Can understand; and he watched her hand reaching him
And knew all existence
And the canvas were one fixed space.

IN THE BURIED NIGHT

They knocked five times at the door
In the buried night.
Open hands or furious fists
Thundered that house where I still forget.

Open? To whom at this hour of night?

And pressing my ear to the wood,
I hardly dared to breathe.
Outside, the wind
Flattening undergowth, beheading stones,
Angrily tore the air.

At last I spoke: 'What's happening? Who are you?'

No one answered.
In dark restiveness a shadow grew
Gradually closer and clearer
As though my heart pounded in the walls,
And in that dark, only
Fear, questions,
Five knocks and their huge hands.

THE SECRET OF THE SPRINGS

Because we shall always know without knowing
That it will be a slow suffering,
A sea stopped
Like water scattering through mazes of smoke,
Blurred stairways
Where eyes would grow in shadow
And tumultuously break
An awakened tear on the verge of the void.
In that clear forest without answers,
There where love closes your eyes
And the stars light up
Like deer that know the wind's direction,
We would hear the unicorn's magic passing
Through the chaste flowers
Of the first lights of night,
That hour when the springs
Offer a hidden language, tenuous and untouched,
With which to interpret
The fresh decisions of death.

COBRA

On the shifting desert sands
Grain by grain her scaly smoothness stands.

Queen and flower of stone, tattooed with fear
Of superstition and omen,
Her myth's malignant thirst swells.

Watch her in her electric cadence
With her dance's hypnotic truce,
Brandishing abyss between her forked tongue.

Her eyes are sirocco mist,
Sphinx blood growing in your gaze
Through which her slow sentence slithers.

THE WARRIOR'S DEATH

Taken by surprise, he fell flat on the ground.
His spilt blood momentarily
Dazzled the mud. He saw the greenery
Slowly stalk the forest of the dark
In the brightest radiance of the day.
From his wound a freshness of flags rose,
The determined weapons invaded the wind,
The blue cavalry slipping
Among the thickets and stones.
His fiery actions seared the sun,
The white-hot metals vibrated soundlessly.
He went on listening to his blood fill the distances,
Clutching to the end the watchful steel.
A cold cloud of smoke brought his victory.
He happily died, smiling at the trees,
For his last dream avenged him.

DEEP WATERS

The water extends wearier and blacker,
The sea ending and filling without time.
I sink the long oars tenaciously down, muffled
In a dark splashing
That invokes and leads memory astray.
I row with a power buried in itself
Asking if it's made of fear or absence.
Farther and farther the long flowing persists,
And the hard, black water, unending night,
And the oars of dense, black water
And the swift circle of the deep.
Now my arms are water among the waters,
And I row and row for ever
And for never, never, I row
In the night's last gulf
And in its hidden waters.

THE TUNNEL OF DEATH
WITH MORE EYES

Strange hold of the night extending
A tunnel of eyes within my eyes.
Relentless and certain, death once again
Looms in each eye.
A stealthy call spreads,
Invading my blood with blindness from the abyss.
I can still hear its black dispersion grow.
It unleashes a blizzard of far-away voices
And suddenly the sea is soundless.
                                    Silences yawn
With the rage of the cold on the reef.
From its surf emerges the crater of a barren sun.
Successive depth well-deep in my eyes,
Adding more eyes to the tunnel of death.

THE CAPTIVE STATUES

He woke in a valley of statues,
Knowing he was one more statue facing the void.
A dahlia of shadow grew
In the muteness of his stony eyes.
The condemned sky was colourless.
The present escaped with a dark
Gust of words, leaving only wakes
Murmuring their lost beginnings.
Descending cloud banks blotted out his world.
Memories also fled without resignation.
Fingers of loneliness and unavoidable rock
Seized his arm. From that still mouth
A stray voice of time cast him aside:
' . . . And you shall remain in the flow of man,
Ignored and captive in his memory
Like what is not alive and never dies.'

DEATH SHALL COME
AND IT WILL HAVE THE RAIN

The rain falls indelibly with the doggedness
Of centuries, seeping through a tumult of anguish.
It falls funereal and exact, monotonous, obsessed,
Silencing all light, opening furrows
Of shadow in the sunny memory of the warbling of birds.
It soaks wood and innocence
With a violent gasping that burns and coats them
With a breath of lasting ash.

The rain falls, eating into eyelids, fruits, distances,
Bleeding the deep pulp of the earth.
Rain, rain carrying out condemnations and revenges
Of forgotten races, of promises and passions
Hopelessly unfulfilled.
The rain falls with that dull sterility of useless things,
Cutting off audiences from what shines and sings.

The rain falls, robbing us of the sun and its remembrance
With a rolling of stones and whispers of ruin.
Sleepwalking, spurious rain, exerminating water
And the rebellious hand clutching to the limit,
Managing to wipe out the world of eyes
And leave the livid, lifeless
Mist of the most helpless state.

The rain falls with that gradual agony
Of poison lying in wait on the body's paths
And meticulously forcing its way through
With terrifying teeth and mathematics
                              frozen with destruction.

The slithering rain falls, lighting up torrents,
Making us shrouds of mercury,
Mire of an airy lake
In which only unmercifulness can flourish.
It falls blind, burning and turbulent
With the ravenous image of repeated crimes
In death's red instant.

from
The Gifts of Earth
Los dones de la tierra
(1984)

THE ANCESTRY OF FIRE

I

You were born in the volcano's thunder,
In the seething slashes of lightning,
When the hidden caves of men
Still did not exist on Earth.
In the distant dawn of that undated age,
You were an unknown god, the cruellest, the most fateful.
Your image of amaranth devoured all
And your magnetic tongue cut
Minerals and forests and bellowings of shadow
To go on eating them up in the lethal rose
Of your fathomless womb.

Because man thinks, he began to know you.
From your unsheltered loneliness,
In his efforts he learned to summon you
With wood, with tinder, with unfailing flint.
In his savage hands you reappeared
Like a solar sword against the winter
And you stopped being the holy wrath,
Corolla of rancour, eagle at ground level,
Mirror swallowing up its images,
Eye through which hells gaze.

They went on reducing you without your noticing.
They locked you in arrows, harquebuses and bombs
And in all the tattoos of war and crime
Like a sure herald of death.
You crossed centuries, continents and rags
Hoisting a howl of fury and misfortune.
You were the gift of destructive force,
Blind scythe, leprosy of the winds,
Impenetrable forest of dark horsemen
Waving flags of murdered blood
In the dreary history of human suffering.

II

But fire is a journey that never halts,
A space by which we are beheld and bared,
Fleeing toward the chance of the remote
With the thirst of a perpetual happening.
Time and transformation, knot untying
Toward the transparence of the unanimous
As it changes matter and its fate.

134

If you put your face close to silence
You'll hear it breathe, lifting light resonances.
Don't be surprised that, modest and familiar, it fits
In the dense and briefest outcry of a match,
Growing in our fingers like a swift poppy
To be light, a song of fireplaces
Or the protective imp of any dance.

III

Fire, standing star, round writing,
Splendour reviving in my chest,
In your forms I find the woman that engulfs me
With a sea of orange trees melting
In my stormy constellations.
I invoke you, set you alight, multiply you.
Open your dizzy vine and speak
With your vehement truth and might.

Tireless, in my poem you were
Life's most intense symbol,
Memory reborn in all its density,
But today I sing to you come down from time
To the seized instant of this day
To live your victory with me.

THE WATERS' FASCINATION

I

The river flows on amidst clear meanderings,
Subsides, gathering and reflecting in its quicksilver
The drowsiness of pine shade,
The awesome summer's swirling aromas.
In its waters the slightest splashing can be heard.
White sails seem to linger
In the siesta's burning denseness
Like mirages or visions.

Now bees suck their fervours
In the magnolia's open flowers.
A sparrow's flight disappears
From the languid gaze, absorbed.
Clouds turning into bright rocks
Adrift in another river higher and clearer.
The light's fullness in its lucid home.
Teeming music of reflections.
All is multifarious life, constant event.

Dense waters nearly asleep, blues of gold,
From your enraptured bubbling
Ancestral sorceries unfold,
Primal fragrances,
Unfound touches of the breeze.
Noises and trilling fall silent, overcome with heat
By the instant's inertia and blindness.
Minutes of dreams and symbols.
Ataraxia. Branchworks of reflections
Release lived memories, longed for
But ever imprisoned in a distant sorrow.

A torrent of suns rains down
Its impregnable weight upon the silt.
Lethargies emerge from their fiery cores.
They enlarge and permeate the visible.
This heat strips, the light, too, stifles.

Water softens its rings.
Remains motionless in its expanse
Like a shore being born:
The promised crystalline earth.
It seems furrowed from the depths
By a clarity barely hinted
In which beings and shadows are foreseen,
Perhaps not born but, yes, fated
For the fixed flux.

II

At a command from earth,
Angry insistent drums beat
From one mysterious epicentre.
The landscape drops abruptly
As though searching for its dark bowels.

Water rises, dazzled,
Bursts leaping, breaking out of its volume
Like a frightened creeper
Extending countless mirrors over meadow.
The grass, still absorbed in its verdant
Chrysalis, tries vainly to flee
In order to reach its yearning:
To be blue with air.

Water floods all, the roving water,
Wild, pure, sparkling, untamed water.
Maybe it escapes from itself,
Runs as though wanting to spend itself, die out
In a greater dream:
Embrace new worlds,
Own and seed them with rebellious love.

And it leaps among stone
And in the green laziness of toads
Surprises the bushes in their merriment,
Rings enraged round oak groves,
Licks their trunks, jumps on their branches,
Raving, crowning the treetops with foam,
And, pressing them, binds and frees,
Relegates, covering and turning them
Into bewitched beings, submerged.

Nothing sets boundaries to its winged force,
And so it reaches the very border of the slope,
And leaps without thinking,
And gracefully hurtles into emptiness,
And suddenly turns into a waterfall,
Inventing a new light
That multiplies the rainbow's seven fountains.

III

The water blessed by the light,
In a nuptial flight
To marry air and earth,

Runs through the clear vastness
Yoked to new wind, new light,
And falls sprouting and spreading intact.
Now its defiance is fusion, love,
A constant melody to the calm,
And it seeks only its deep way:
To be a given present to all creation.

The blinded water crosses the limits
Of the proud solstice and flows over the world.
Redeeming and joyful, it turns domestic,
Lighting up the whiteness of wash basins,
Slipping bodiless between fingers,
Releasing itself whole.
And it plays, cleanses and exalts man
Who installs it in slender pitchers and vases,
Gem of radiance, glad touch,
That yearned-for moisture of the lips.

And it lives with man and clouds,
With the earth, the flowers and the fauna,
Its rippling, confident dream
Of fulfilling a final fate:
To be life among lives
Till it joins its flowing to the deep sea,
There where death is part of life,
And the sea is end and beginning,
Creative time, sheer light
Of a God inhabiting us forever.

from
Only the Hand
That Writes You Dies
Sólo muere la mano
que te escribe
(1988)

THE HAND THAT WRITES YOU
Homage to Poetry

They are not history, dates, the hours we embrace,
Not even a handful of words
Or flocks of images in eloquent air.
From my forehead springs your name's flow,
And in that still water staring at you
From the past, you live always the way you were,
Unburnt by the years.

I sketch your snowy profile, signs
Dictated by winter's bleak truth.
White laughter, birches, slow fascination,
Time without time, days in night,
Sun returning to its fountainhead of aromas
Beside the cabin's tamed fire.

The world dissolves in your gaze,
The page longing to keep you
In an eternity that aches and stays.

Only the hand that writes you dies.

THE AIR'S AQUARIUM

In the sun's hollow, he lingers, engrossed:
A far-off murmur draws the infinite near,
That whining radiates a strange nostalgia.
They are memories the wind brings from who knows where.

He glimpses a blazing sway of laurels
And in their echoes of shadow, the air's aquarium.
The shining fish weighing
On the green current of the breeze.

He hears the bright zigzag of their constellations
In another space within space,
Seeding and source of all the words
Exalting the energy of the cosmos.

Each root, body or star is a tiny fish
Turning in the bowl of its own galaxy.
Each universe another little fish
From the countless infinite number.

None can reach or decode
This music. It's felt by the soul of things
Like that wandering man who is moved
Listening to the copse of the stars.

OCE—K

HEARD FACES

I sleep and barely sleep beneath the autumn stars.
All the trees live in my closed eyes
Flowing with their rains and ancient echoes.
The wind in the density shakes
Through the shadows with scattered presences,
The frost's vapour breathes, grows
In the deep branches' disturbance.

With the tangible sorrow of night,
With its exhausted fury in the voice of the leaves,
Whispering words I cannot catch,
Each star brings me the faces of my dead.
Their voices slip over sleeping mirrors,
The wood silences their footsteps,
I am called by their grief's dark loneliness.

They throb in my papers and clothes,
Read my dreams, protect my vigil.
I foresee them, tenuous, powerful and confiding
For they must wait for me on the silent threshold
With the golden bough and lunar arms.

And I stretch out my hands, but they dare not touch me,
For if I wake up, if I fix my gaze
On the core of the shadowy spot,
Hearts without feet, a sunset bleeding
Through misty terraces and smokey valleys
Fading in the flight of all that perishes.

I sleep with the lasting smile of their faces
Watching over my waiting, guarding my lineage.

AGAINST THE LIGHT

Against the light of a glass
The landscape halted.
      An oasis of despair
In joy still shone.
Window and snow combining beyond winter
Toward unseen time — departed.

Suddenly I saw so many years darken
In the faltering flight of a leaf.
And when I touched that ground, then I knew its age,
The age of its world, that of all possible
Coming, uncreated worlds,
The never, never more of beauty
Growing obsessed inside her body.

Against the light of a glass
I saw again the landscape unfold
With all the joyfulness prevailing
In the first tear of resignation.

THE FLOOD
OF THIS BEAUTIFUL WOMAN

Her arrival was announced by the fit,
The riot of flesh in my poem.

But what treatment, what writing would be enough
So that her lascivious castanets would not escape,
Nor the smoothness be silenced between my hands
Or the rhythmic beating of her breaker?

I wanted to be cane planted in her streambed
And caressed by the waters
From the cavity of her current,
Or the tiger climbing the greediest pulp
Of the Y or the T on an exhausted couch
Where one reaches the peak of a prolonged privilege.

I dream in this poem of an endless book
To relieve the flood of this beautiful woman.
How many pages on so many occasions
Her whim lifts in my desire.

Neither rancour nor glowing envy
Do I want to wake in your memory,
For, though you ask, I won't give you
The key to her name, nor the dream of her bed,
Nor the scorching thirst for her river thighs.

THE SWAN AND THE LEOPARD

The leopard leaps suddenly from a sunbeam.
His body splashes against the sun
Of the canebrakes, explosion of desire
In a vibrant slant of undergrowth and claws.

The swan flows sleeplessly through the lake.
Over her smooth gliding a stroke of lightning
Stands alert, the silent angel of the dark,
The fleeting langour of music.

They sense each other, fascinated, like two avalanches
Of snow beneath the desert's convulsive sun.
The gold of death, the blood of light,
The unexpected surf against the last horizon.

But the swan's clear wake
Is not the stricken water of the jungle.
They are two different times, two distant
Places joined by a moment's chance
With the glistening of dreams in the word.

THE DEAD MAN I WILL BE

I am hardly questioned by the dead man I will be.
Maybe when he re-emerges from the wilderness of mist,
I will say of those days that emptied my eyes:
You went on dissolving in my pages
Like sand swallowed by sea.
But if everything the air devours is oblivion,
Why should my poems then concern me,
Their brief juice of years, if I shall not be with me?
And you words, images, visions
Cut from the pain and light of life,
You dug an eternal obsession in my time.
Maybe you will assert, though I see it no longer,
That there was a precise fire in my writing,
The cruelty of a darkened fate,
Something of beauty, that feeling, different
For those that hear me still with pristine eyes.

THE CONSTANT CHORD

I know you're the fire's smoothness and its branches,
The feline elegance of the mist,
Unexpected spring, growing till gushing,
Melting me in the spell where I am plunged
Beyond death and its oblivion.
I want to kiss your statuesque infinitude,
Drink you and drown in its other side
Of light and night and dream surprised in flame,
Stretch the skin of vehemence from ecstasy.
Exact craving groping over your contours,
Emerging in the currents of your coast
To install the diamond day.
Your white fire is pulp between my lips.
My back is the whispering of your fingers.
Your hips so slow, so deep in mine
Like a long, piercing chord
Leading life to its source.
Forceful attack on space.
Prow where desires explode.
Quivering roundness, cardinal upheaval,
Spurt of light, clarity's everlasting orgy
Inaugurating in your womb the primal hour.
Word's horizon reincarnated from nothingness
Like shreds of water drawn to the solar magnet.
Your neck is a column where a star rises
Till you go back to your staring eyes
And are the certainty that welcomes and thrills.
Thirst, inner comet, unavoidable giddiness
Rescued surf overwhelming the gale,
And you, like it, ring yourself wholly in my arms.
Your touch enhances me till forgetting.
In my infinite yearning, your infinite breeds
Blue fertility, water and its mystery.
Sign and summit in your lips, the choice
For which I wager the world. We are a hand
Seizing the flight that is reached and crowned
In the total dream of its design.
You persist in my gaze, you go on boundlessly
Being born from your eyes, from the sea
Hurtling down in your ceaseless body.

A BLOOD REASON

In your tongue the reddest currents coil,
Strength and purity of instinct.
Every caress is grass and each fullness
Is now a beginning, a blood reason.

The night's convulsive flood
Revives and brims over in your hips.
Even the sun beneath your skin dazzles
The mineral breath of want.

You swirl among branches, so full of cadences,
Quivering in the tremor of a whirlwhind ensnared.
A magnetic heart attracts us to its core.
Caressing shadows, we listen to its blaze.

Your body, like time, always flows.
Without your lessening it, it sums up the universe.
It is the honey since birth and gift to its owner,
Unstained by interest, uneffaced by eternity.
It has lingered in my eyes like ocean light.

FABLE OF TWO CASTAWAYS

They were two castaways of long exposures,
Two pale travellers of failure
Whose vertigo was cleaved by the chimera.
Error opened a constant current to a vast terrain
Where helplessly they wandered lost.
Sadly, with a flame of misery
In the ice and disorder of their eyes,
Before chance brought them together,
They had cruelly learned perhaps
The most horrible word: survival.

So given to the ritual of loss,
They extolled each other deep as sea and rocks
Amidst the blue violence of summer.
Beneath a round space of planets,
Motionless seasons plowed.
Desire and its abyss magnetized their course.
From the cold of salt and its dark bellowing
And always from the threatening past
Sharks of shadow appeared.

They made storms and snows come late.
And the chimera no longer wanted to be chimera.
It was the island, the dream, the long nights,
The bodies kindled with wonder,
The house built with wide-open eyes.
There the greenery, the intimate haven.
Even the bougainvillaea was a fountain
That grew tenaciously by the window.
On stormy nights, through the willows,
Hate slipped by with its lamentations,
The immemorial rain, its lurking misfortune.
But they hooked each other like stone in the claw.
They hugged, asking for each other, yearning, spilling.
They were their own blaze, their boundless cabin.
And always that unlucky passion encrusted
In the bitterest pain of their bodies
Or in the waking vision of their closed eyes.

From the geology of thirst
Till the water securing all space,
They watched the forest thickness
With its fire raised in the final origin.
The wind gathered in the branches
Messenger cawings, knotted memories
That were gradually, stealthily unravelling
The fauna and refulgence of the open.

They went back to believing in other years
Where freedom was uncertainty.

In the air, a distant perfume of magnolias,
The abolished dream of space,
A time where none existed.

Guilty or innocent, their looks never managed to meet.

The island faded away like the flight that sways
And unexpectedly grows smaller
Till it becomes almost a dot and disappears.

THE WOUNDED NEGATION

After the wholeness of doubt
Or in the wounded negation
Where we erase ourselves in our unknowing,
I persist with the intermittent strangeness
Recognized when falling into the lost.
Then desolate is the memory of the word
And you emerge with echoes tormenting mist.

And I cling to the rowing of our bodies.
There where the driest
Pleading words sparkle,
Fear nests, extending extermination
Among the beauties of fever
And refulgence of teeth tarnishing
And tightening a forsaken fervour.

In the shadow,
A white-hot melting point
To sink into the skin
Calling me beneath your skin,
And to find in that kingdom
The light of your roads pursued
In the ritual dark of a desert.

In this darkness, all your flesh,
A white mirage for my thirst.
Its most vehement clock soaking
The forgetting of a pleasure suffering its own forgetting,
The dunes and tides panting
Their everlasting maze among what's dead.
Life this way is not mine, nor this pain yours.
In some terrain deep within
We must find each other like water in its bed
Tumultuously rising to celebrate its union.

I love the light of our pupils reflected.
I rise among their gusts and narrow into your odour
Of lush honeysuckle and warm honey,
And a troubled pleasure undermines me.
And our lips are sacrifice, fusing, cracking
To feel the drunkenness of the earthly,
A fire suddenly slipping into the brain,
Deepening desire in instinct.

Your clear lechery tightens
Towards a place belonging to the body rediscovered,
Where the womb is a maddened sun,
To feel it and be enchased within
Like a fist locking its treasure.
I am a mirror carried away by a tropic
Of lustful vines, of rocks where anxiety
Strips, sows and reunites
And starts to reveal itself when it forgets.

And if I look behind and foresee you
In the unsuspected spilling of sorrow,
I hear the wandering murmur of your love in others
Across the earth in which we grow.
This landscape of ours scorched
Its shadows into your eyes, just as now you slowly
Etch your eyes into mine to feel once more
That love is stubborn and its damage stronger still.

I remember you in the naked night of this room
With your swing of swaying branches.
You tucked your knees beneath your face,
And hoisted in your lips a distant smile
That looked at me, calling with a single craving.

And you were my savage skin, tenderness tendered,
Glow of felinity and lightest honey.
Most fragrant warmth and always a promise.
Immune contradiction of sensuality
Where an instant is flower and idolatry,
Lunar deity wheeling subdued
Beneath the red stars of summer.

Wisdom: your body's word.
It tells me its history of confusion and chaos,
Images injured and mirages
Quenching the aroma of a former innocence.
You were innocence regained
With steadily greater ire in your errors
Are in your ascendent way of looking at me,
Or of remaining absorbed and certain
As if words and memories had fled from you
And you were only that kiss yoking me
To the risk and fullness of the absolute.

Men of tedium, pressed by the thirst of possessing you,
Passed with a silent gallop through your years
Without managing to be oasis in your memory.
They did not stain the fountain of your flesh,
They did not spoil the indecisive search,
Nor the dreams of that loneliness
Spying in the distance its chimera.

The most orphaned grief rises
Because you grew away from my wandering,
Because you burned in the open air
What you give me now
With the prodigal hands death will steal.

From a tight and vanquished pain, flickering
Moon on your naked feet, arrive
A smell of lavender, a bewitching breeze,
The unending halo on the skin of miracle.
But I still have no idea what different brightness,
What black waters of stars, what far-off music
Makes you ripple in my shadow and what silence
Is left in the face of my defenselessness in loving you.

I can no longer brandish pleas or fears,
For I love you as if I were growing again
With all my errors learned,
Behind that door left ajar by dread,
Listening to my footsteps in the cellars
Of the wind amidst hallucinate night,
Turning through the black portals of emptiness,
With empty orbits,
Where the emptiness devoured the eyes
Of love and all its origins.

My memory is only a frozen impulse
Continuing in your impossible inexistence.
The ocean's silence would not be enough
For me to forget and deny you.
Just one thought
Is now all my life till death.

MEMORY OF A FRAGRANCE

In the birds' brief silences
Night half-opened its dark syllables.
I left the edge of the road behind
To hear the rustic heart of earth.
Invisible presences sailed
A dense air, an air of aromas.
I remained alert, decoding
The leaves' echo, that warm thickness
Begun by a whisper of blackbirds.
Hardly even a breath, a distant trace,
An impulse that would be flag and astrolabe,
Wild in the honey of shadow.
But it wasn't the steely freshness of thyme,
Nor the snowy bonfire of the cherry tree
Or the sensuality of magnolia and rose.
I closed my eyes to smell enigmas
Intoxicating me from the mists.
Their stars arrived with a seething of crystals,
Fireflies of water so sinuous and white,
The swaying of submerged pines,
The passion of the rising nouns.
All language hearing the intact melody
Rooting its uneasiness in memory.
I perceive a weight of thirsty branches,
Bubblings or the clean slipping
Of some thighs weaving in the grass.
Now the moon hangs from their bodies
As though a bright brush wiped them away,
And that aroma demolishes my youth burnt out,
Stubbornly abolished by the years.

THE PROMISE

And when one day I turn into topsoil,
Barely a stubble field that no one knows,
Or into dawn revolving through the clouds,
Two drops of water will still want to refuse
Relentless and lasting destruction.
My eyes. I know they will go on gazing at
Our world, an island, this shore of sun.
Just as now, their tears will fall facing the shadow
Of a lazy willow on Mount Lentiscal
When they remember all I loved
Between the sea and the land of life.

FOREST BOOKS

Special Collection
THE NAKED MACHINE Selected poems of Matthias Johannessen.
Translated from the *Icelandic* by Marshall Brement.
0 948259 44 2 cloth £7.95   0 948259 43 4 paper £5.95   96p pages
ON THE CUTTING EDGE Selected poems of Justo Jorge Padrón.
Translated from the *Spanish* by Louis Bourne.
0 948259 42 6 paper £7.95   176 pages
ROOM WITHOUT WALLS Selected poems of Bo Carpelan.
Translated from the *Swedish* by Ann Borne.
0 948259 08 6 paper £6.95   144 pages. Illustrated
CALL YOURSELF ALIVE The love poems of Nina Cassian.
Translated from the *Romanian* by Andrea Deletant and Brenda Walker.
Introduction by Fleur Adcock.
0 948259 38 8 paper £5.95.   96 pages. Illustrated
RUNNING TO THE SHROUDS Six sea stories of Konstantin Stanyukovich.
Translated from the *Russian* by Neil Parsons.
0 948259 04 3 paper £5.95   112 pages.

East European Series
FOOTPRINTS OF THE WIND Selected poems of Mateya Matevski.
Translated from the *Macedonian* by Ewald Osers. Introduction by Robin Skelton.
0 948259 41 8 paper £6.95   96 pages. Illustrated
ARIADNE'S THREAD An anthology of contemporary Polish Women poets.
Translated from the *Polish* by Susan Bassnett and Piotr Kuhiwczak.
0 948259 45 0 paper £6.95   96 pages.
POETS OF BULGARIA An anthology of contemporary Bulgarian poets.
Edited by William Meredith. Introduction by Alan Brownjohn.
0 948259 39 6 paper £6.95   112 pages.
THE ROAD TO FREEDOM by Geo Milev. Translated from the *Bulgarian* by Ewald Osers.
UNESCO collection of representative works.
0 948259 40 X paper £6.95   96 pages. Illustrated.
STOLEN FIRE Selected poems by Lyubomir Levchev.
Translated from the *Bulgarian* by Ewald Osers. Introduction by John Balaban.
UNESCO collection of representative works.
0 948259 04 3 paper £5.95   112 pages. Illustrated
AN ANTHOLOGY OF CONTEMPORARY ROMANIAN POETRY
Translated by Andrea Deletant and Brenda Walker.
0 9509487 4 8 paper £5.00   112 pages.
GATES OF THE MOMENT Selected poems of Ion Stoica.
Translated from the *Romanian* by Brenda Walker and Andrea Deletant.
Dual text with cassette.
0 9509487 0 5 paper £5.00   126 pages   Cassette £3.50 plus VAT
SILENT VOICES An anthology of contemporary Romanian women poets.
Translated by Andrea Deletant and Brenda Walker. Introduction by Fleur Adcock.
0 948259 03 5 paper £6.95   172 pages.
EXILE ON A PEPPERCORN Selected poems of Mircea Dinescu.
Translated from the *Romanian* by Andrea Deletant and Brenda Walker.
0 948259 00 0 paper £5.95.   96 pages. Illustrated.
LET'S TALK ABOUT THE WEATHER Selected poems of Marin Sorescu.
Translated from the *Romanian* by Andrea Deletant and Brenda Walker.
0 9509487 8 0 paper £5.95   96 pages.
THE THIRST OF THE SALT MOUNTAIN Three plays by Marin Sorescu
(Jonah, The Verger, and the Matrix).
Translated from the *Romanian* by Andrea Deletant and Brenda Walker.
0 9509487 5 6 paper £6.95   124 pages. Illustrated
VLAD DRACULA THE IMPALER A play by Marin Sorescu.
Translated from the *Romanian* by Dennis Deletant.
0 948259 07 8 paper £6.95   112 pages. Illustrated.

Fun Series
JOUSTS OF APHRODITE Poems collected from the Greek Anthology Book V.
Translated from the *Greek* into modern English by Michael Kelly.
0 948259 05 1 £6.95   0 948259 34 5 paper £4.95   96 pages.